New Crops
from
Old Fields

Eight Medievalist Poets

Editor Oz Hardwick

Stairwell Books

Published by Stairwell Books
70 Barbara Drive
Norwalk
CT 06851 USA

161 Lowther Street
York
YO31 1LZ

New Crops from Old Fields©2015, The Authors and Stairwell Books

ISBN: 978-1-939269-31-7

Printed and bound in the UK by Russell Press
Layout design: Alan Gillott
Cover Photograph: Oz Hardwick
Edited by Oz Hardwick

Proceeds from this book will be donated to The West of England MS Therapy Centre.

        www.mstherapybristol.org.uk

Table of Contents

Introduction

> For out of olde feldes, as men seith,
> Cometh al this new corn fro yeer to yere;
> And out of olde bokes, in good feith,
> Cometh al this newe science that men lere.[1]

So says Geoffrey Chaucer near the start of *The Parlement of Foules*. It's an assertion we can trust: Chaucer may have been 'The Father of English Poetry,' but he was no stranger to raising and harvesting his bumper crop from the literary fields which others had previously tilled. Such, indeed, is the nature of all creative endeavour for, whether we wish to build steadily upon the works of others, or seek a radical break with tradition, we must first immerse ourselves within the work of those who have gone before us. The writers gathered in this volume have a particular engagement with the field of medieval literature, each, for their own diverse reasons, having dedicated much of their professional life to date to its study.

There is an apparent paradox inherent in our relationship with the Western Middle Ages. As a subject of scholarly investigation, it is not the most immediately attractive to the would-be student. Survival of material culture is patchy and written sources range from a bit tricky to thoroughly incomprehensible without diligent application. And when we do overcome these barriers, what we find, more often than not, is a world of disease, war, inequality and intolerant prejudice. Yet, as Tison Pugh and Angela Jane Weisl note, 'despite the unpleasantness of historical reality, the Middle Ages is magic.'[2] Whether it's Disney or Monty Python, King Arthur will draw us to the cinema, while Rosemary Sutcliffe or Bernard Cornwell will keep us turning the pages – and who can resist a re-enacted joust? And whether it's a ruined

---

[1] Geoffrey Chaucer, *The Parlement of Foules*, in *The Riverside Chaucer*, 3rd edn., ed. Larry D. Benson (Oxford: OUP, 1987), ll. 22-5.

[2] Tison Pugh and Angela Jane Weisl, *Medievalisms* (Oxford: Routledge, 2013), p. 1.

castle or abbey, or a Renaissance Fair, there's never a shortage of punters wishing to immerse themselves, at least temporarily, in the (suitably sanitised) Middle Ages. This enthusiasm for imaginatively revisiting and recreating the medieval past is not a new phenomenon. Indeed, as Umberto Eco observes, 'Modern ages have revisited the Middle Ages from the moment when, according to historical handbooks, they came to an end.'[3] By the close of the sixteenth century, Spenser was weaving Arthurian matter into his *Faerie Queene* (1590, 1596), while by the close of the nineteenth, Burne-Jones, Morris and Dearle were weaving it into their tapestries (1891-94).

The growth of antiquarianism from the late eighteenth century led to an ostensibly more objective view of the Middle Ages, but it cannot be overlooked that one of the key drivers for this engagement with history, in Britain at least, was to propound a sense of cultural and political identity distinct from that of revolutionary Europe. Consequently, the study of medieval history, as with all investigation of the past, vividly illustrates Nietzsche's dictum that, 'there are no facts, only interpretations.'[4] It may be seen, then, that whether they are elucidating the finer points of the circumstances surrounding the signing of Magna Carta (1215), or dressing up as fanciful champions for the Eglinton Tournament (1839), the 'merry company' of medievalists who have ploughed this field for the past half century or thereabouts, have all, to varying degrees – and with varying degrees of intentionality – refashioned the Middle Ages in their own image. Eco offers 'Ten Little Middle Ages' for our consideration.[5] The details – and indeed the number – belong to another discussion, but the principle of his argument is pertinent

---

[3] Umberto Eco, *Travels in Hyper-reality* (London: Picador, 1987), p. 65.

[4] The observation is made a number of times in Nietzsche's unpublished notebooks of the 1880s. See http://plato.stanford.edu/entries/nietzsche/ [accessed 23 February 2015]

[5] Eco, *Travels*, p. 68.

to the poems in this collection: whatever Middle Ages are invoked, they constitute a mirror, which reflects not only the past, but also the present.

From Spencer's political critique in *The Faerie Queene* to Douglas Oliver's satire on Thatcher's Britain in *The Infant and the Pearl* (1985), via the erotically-charged aestheticism of Rossetti's 'The Blessed Damosel' (1850), the dark psychological self-interrogation of Browning's 'Childe Roland to the Dark Tower Came' (1855), and Hopkins' redeployment of Anglo-Saxon alliteration, there has been a rich and infinitely varied strain of medievalist poetry in English. When planning the current collection, I approached medieval scholars who, as I have discovered, sometimes quite by chance, also have distinctive poetic voices, and asked them not only to submit a selection of poems, but also a short introduction on the way(s) in which they respond creatively to the Middle Ages. These introductions are as varied as the poems, and I hope that the reader will find them as illuminating and stimulating as I do, revealing still more 'Little Middle Ages' to explore.

I would like to thank the contributors to this collection for taking the time to reflect upon and share the points at which aspects of their relationship with the Middle Ages, often kept separate by disciplinary divisions still frequently imposed within academia, fuse into creative expression. Further, on behalf of all of us, I would like to offer heartfelt thanks to colleagues, past teachers, and students, along with, 'Chaucer, Langland, Douglas, Dunbar, with all (their) brother Anons,'[6] – and not forgetting their sister Anons, too – for their continued inspiration.

Prof Paul Hardwick
Leeds February 2015

Oz Hardwick
London June 1381

---

[6] 'Ode to the Medieval Poets,' in W. H. Auden, *Collected Poems*, revised edn., ed. Edward Mendelson (London: Faber and Faber, 1991), p. 863.

Jane Beal

The Million-Dollar Challenge: Of Pilgrimage and Poetry...

As the fall semester of 2006 began, the faculty of Wheaton College divided into small groups to go out to dinner. I was in a group that went to a Japanese restaurant where we enjoyed miso soup, fresh sushi, teriyaki chicken, steamed rice, tempura vegetables and, if memory serves, green tea ice-cream. To facilitate conversation, and help everyone get to know one another, our host asked a question: "If you had a million dollars, and you couldn't donate it to charity but had to spend it on yourself, what would you do?" I knew immediately, and I was brimming with excitement when I shared my idea: I would go on a pilgrimage like medieval people did, I said, from Santiago de Compostela in Spain to Rome in Italy to Jerusalem in Israel.

After dinner, I realized that I did not need a million dollars to do this.

In the summer of 2007, the Wheaton College Human Needs and Global Resources program asked me to visit a student intern, whose work I was supervising, on-site in Moldova. I agreed. Although the program could not pay me for this service, the director arranged for me to have a three-day layover in Rome on the way back. So I began my pilgrimage *in media res*. The following summer, I was turning thirty-three years old, and I asked myself, "What would Jesus do?" When he was my age, he went to Jerusalem, and so I went, too. In the summer of 2009, I went to Spain, and I made my way by train from Madrid to Toledo to Avila to Leon and finally to Santiago de Compostela, where I ended my pilgrimage at the beginning of the medieval route.

I ended at the beginning. But I knew then, as now, that my journey had not really reached its conclusion. My whole life is a pilgrimage.

Medieval people often saw their lives as a pilgrimage, too, and this world-view is reflected in the major literature of the late-medieval English period: Chaucer's episodic *Canterbury Tales*, the spiritual autobiography of Margery Kempe, the morality play *Everyman* (to name only three examples). Certainly I have written poetry about my pilgrimage experience in Rome, Jerusalem, and Santiago, but at a much more fundamental level, pilgrimage is a metaphor for this life that deeply informs my poetry. Life is a journey, yes, but one infused with spiritual purpose and directed toward holy places on earth that will eventually lead, by God's grace, to my true heavenly home.

That said, I admit there is somewhat of a division between my literary scholarship (analysis) and my creative writing (synthesis). These two partially, but not completely, relate to one another. Perhaps only 10% of my poetry has direct allusions to medieval literature. Yet the idea of pilgrimage forms a bridge between the two creative endeavors.

For me, the practice of translation also deepens meaning in both fields, critical and creative – and, as Walter Benjamin might agree, I have discovered that more is found than lost in translation. As a medievalist, I must translate older forms of English, French, and Latin (and occasionally Hebrew and Greek) into modern English. As a lyric poet, I must translate emotion and the memory of experience from my heart to my reader. In both cases, translation is a key that opens new doors.

My work with the Middle English dream vision poem *Pearl* has called forth from me the most elaborate translation efforts, from a fully annotated translation into contemporary English to a monograph interpreting the poem to a co-edited collection of essays on how to teach the poem at the collegiate level. It has branched into a fascination with the influence of *Pearl* on J.R.R. Tolkien's legend of Beren and Lúthien. The structure of *Pearl* relates to the structure of "Sanctuary" (the title poem of my first published collection); I suspect more allusions from *Pearl* will find their way into my future poems.

My study of medieval literature inspires my poetry in other ways as well. It informs my perceptions of nature ("Filia Magistri in the Midwest" and "On Seeing Reynard Unexpectedly"), allows me to express emotion through dramatic monologues articulated by people or literary characters of the Middle Ages ("Caedmon Remembers," "Lady Herodis Listens to Sir Orfeo," "Dante Journeys toward Heaven"), and motivates me to recall my own lived experience of the geography and architecture of places in the world that are, historically speaking, ancient or medieval, like the Coliseum in Rome, the walls of Avila, the Cathedral of Santiago de Compostela ("The Eternal City" and "Shadow-Pilgrim of the Cathedral").

The poems I include in this anthology should be comprehensible to most medievalists who study literature and, I think, to many general readers as well. It's worth noting that *Filia magistri* (meaning "daughter of the Master") is an abbreviation of Peter Lombard's Latin *Sentences*, Reynard is a fox trickster hero from Old French fable (often satirical in nature), Orfeo and Herodis are characters from the Middle English romance "Sir Orfeo" (in which, unlike the classical Greco-Roman tale, Herodis does return), and Caedmon is the first English poet whose poetry is preserved in English (specifically, as Old English glosses in manuscripts of the Venerable Bede's Latin *Ecclesiastical History*). Dante is, of course, the author of *The Divine Comedy*, a dream vision poem about his spiritual pilgrimage through the hell, purgatory and heaven.

I include three poems from my medieval pilgrimage (2007-2009) here as well. "The Eternal City" consists of three sonnets about significant Roman monuments: the cathedral of San Pietro, the Coliseum, and the Fontana di Trevi. "Questions" consists of real queries posed to me by Jews and Muslims, Israelis and Palestinians, when I traveled in the Holy Land. "The Shadow-Pilgrim of the Cathedral" was inspired by a nighttime visit to one side of the Praza da Obradorio, where two friends, Monica and Fernando, showed me a stone pillar built so that, when the light falls on it in darkness, the shadow of Saint James appears on the walls of the cathedral.

Postscript: "Filia Magistri in the Midwest" first appeared in print as "My friend Franklin is a theologian" in *Ruminate*, "On Seeing Reynard Unexpectedly" in my book *Jazz Birding*, "Lady Herodis Listens to Sir Orfeo" in my book *Magical Poems for Girls*, and "Caedmon Remembers" in *Cantos: A Literature and Arts Journal*. They have been revised for inclusion in this anthology. The other four poems are published here for the first time.

I would like to thank my friend Gary, who celebrated with me the first acceptance of "Filia Magistri" for publication years ago, and who is, in more ways than one, my Orfeo.

Jane Beal

Filia Magistri in the Midwest

My friend Franklin is a theologian.
With care, he studies representations
of Moses in St. Thomas Aquinas,
devout Victorines in medieval France,
Peter Abelard's florid *Sentences,*
and abbreviations like *Filia
magistri,* the daughter of the Master,
(which sounds like a person but is really
a book), and I am listening to him

but I am also looking beyond him
out the window at a tree with new leaves,
green and trembling on the branch in the wind,
as the rain falls from the gray skies and drips
from the leaf-edges to the soil and roots.

Seeing Reynard Unexpectedly

From the roadside,
I see a fair fox chewing
as he stands in tall, green grass—
the forest behind him
goes on forever.

Caedmon Remembers

Hearing the harp, like hearing my enemy's horn,
filled my heart with fear even when I was
longing for heaven to come down into my hands

so I could pray and praise in the company
of men in the mead-hall, those ordinary mortals,
my friends and my kinsmen from whom I fled

to bungle my way to the barn to bed down
with the animals, not expecting the angel, who appeared
and said: *Sing to the Shaper the beginnings of earth and sky!*

Jane Beal

Lady Herodis Listens to Sir Orfeo Sing

When you touch the strings of your harp, when you
lift your voice to sing, our eyes meet across
the distance of the hall, and my heart resonates
to the timbre and the tone of your tenderness.

That magical harp! Your magnificent song!
They awakened me when I slept like the dead
in the house of the Faery-King, his prisoner
in the shadow-world, frozen, until you came.

Under that grafted-tree on a forked path, I lay
when your hand reached out for mine, and gripping hard,
pulled me up out of a dark slumber into light
and led me back to life in Winchester Castle.

You sing a song of healing, and I remember –
you sing a song of love, and I live forever.

Dante Journeys toward Heaven

I was afraid of everything: three
beasts – lion-pride, leopard-lust, wolfish greed –
the mouth of hell, making neutrality
my unmade choice, unbaptized babies lost
in Elysium with righteous heathen,
Francesca damned for her adultery,
men who ate too much, a dog with three mouths,
prodigal sons and selfish priests, wasting
the gifts of God, Furies screaming for blood,
violence, deception, betrayal, death.

But even in the depths of hell, Virgil
told me that the universe once felt love.
When the name of the Lover could not be
spoken, the mercurial angel came
and opened the locked gate of the city.
I gathered leaves under the twisted trees,
met the treasured teacher who touched my hem,
and became strong and courageous, a new
Icarus who did not fall to his death,
but learned that the way up must first go down.

Down past Jason, the demons, and their pitch,
down past the hypocrites and the snake-skins,
down below the pit where the giant lowered
me into the coldest darkness I have
ever known. There I saw a man gnawing
on another's skull, then the three faces
of Lucifer – black, white, and red – mouths fierce
and chewing on the disembodied souls
of traitors who, even in hell, did not
turn from the grief they had caused the world.

Jane Beal

But at last I climbed a ladder made of hair,
each rung a step in contemplation closer
to a stream, a rose of light, and the blessed stars.

The Eternal City

San Pietro

In Rome, the Eternal City, I saw
the great cathedral of San Pietro
built over the circus-hill of Nero,
the catacombs beneath the church, the Papa.
Yes! The popes' tombs engraved with Latin law,
the Christian pilgrims who, in tears, bowed low
amidst medieval treasures aglow
with present promise: the past in the raw –
and I prayed as I listened to the dead,
the faint wind whispering in the shadows,
thinking of how the saints still speak to us.
I prayed to God as I looked up and read
Maiorem gloriam Dei: stone knows
the power of the resurrected Jesus.

Coliseum

In Rome, the Eternal City, I see
the walls of the Coliseum ahead
where beasts, saints, and gladiators once sped,
where Perpetua called the Almighty.
The ancient stones still stand gloriously,
they yet remember the blood that was shed:
the mighty struggles, the victors, the dead,
the arena when it was a wild sea.
Even pebbles cry out praise for the past,
they echo the song Amphion once played,
and they repeat the enduring refrain:
when the great God-man comes again at last,
we will be strong here still, the rocks he made
to bear witness to grace redeeming pain.

Jane Beal

Fontana di Trevi

In Rome, the Eternal City, I will see
the Fontana di Trevi bright with coins
as the splashing water falls and then joins
the light in the pool for eternity.
I will walk on that water fearlessly,
my mighty heart singing to the blood in my veins,
my soul shake off darkness and iron chains
as I enter into the mystery:
there is hope and a future yet to be—
the wolf who mothered Romulus lies down
with the Lamb who made her legendary;
there is the fulfillment of history,
rewards for the righteous, a jeweled crown,
and at the end of time, Christ's victory.

Questions

Where are you from?
  Is this your first time in Israel?
Are you alone or with a group?

Are you married?
  Are you Jewish?
Why aren't you married?

Do you like Israel?
  Isn't Jerusalem beautiful?
Do you want to move here?

Will you come visit me?
  Do you want to go to Ramallah?
Isn't Ramallah beautiful?

Don't you like me?
  Are you afraid of me?
Do you want to go to the Dead Sea?

Have you been to Bethlehem?
  Have you been to the grotto of the Mother's milk?
What gift do you want?

How long are you staying here?
  When can I see you again?
When will you return to Israel?

The Shadow-Pilgrim of the Cathedral of Santiago de Compostela

By the cathedral of Santiago,
a granite pillar also stands and waits,
casting a shadow against the church wall
in the shape of a far-walking pilgrim:

like St. James, a floppy hat on his head,
a wooden stick in his hand for the Way,
and a dried pumpkin gourd full of water
swinging from one end of his journey-stick.

I perceive him there, the shadow-walker,
his white scallop shell hidden from my view,
his whole body leaning against the stones,
his whole soul revealed by a light in the dark.

What shape does the shadow of my life form
when I take my stand in the light of God?

Jane Chance

Medievalist poetry may facilitate an understanding of the modern and postmodern vernacularity of the Middle Ages while concealing the personal. My poems reflect some of my research interests in medieval literature: women's experience as sexual beings, wives, and mothers and, equally, women medievalists' experiences as academics, often involving travel. Given scholars' training to maintain objectivity and the life of the mind, medievalism helps create an imaginary shield against personal revelation. I say 'imaginary,' because the poems, like the medieval artistry they emulate, are fantasy, fantastic and fabulous on the outside, naked truth inside.

One setting conducive to my realization of the medievalistic is Brittany, a province that lays claim historically and culturally to the Middle Ages in its literature. Twelfth-century Marie de France's effeminate hero in her lay, *Lanval*, comes from Brittany, as does the treacherous Lancelot du Lac of so many English and French Arthurian romances. Brittany's architecture and towns or sites inspire three of my poems – the castle of Suscinio, the forest of Broceliande, and the abbey at Rhuys – the last, to which Peter Abelard was exiled, an experience documented in his autobiography.

The medieval French *aventure* (adventure or journey, and also the genre of the romance) depends upon courtly love and chivalry, both of which reappear in modern dress in 'Aventure.' Here I speculate how a young knight might have felt setting out one spring morning on his own to make his name. In one line, I imagine him attending 'knight camp' at the castle of Suscinio in parody of contemporary summer youth camps that offer boys physical training much like that experienced by a medieval page or bachelor knight. So the poem invokes the trappings of medieval aristocratic life in a contemporary world in which both lovers, and not just the second son of an aristocratic family, might worry if there is money enough to marry. I also imagine my own sons, setting out in life in their careers and relationships as if on a quest.

The forest of Broceliande still exists on the map, much visited by tourists. I stayed about fifteen kilometres away in a fourteenth-century castle, which helped to kindle my imagination. In 'The Château de Comper,' the castle seems to speak, although in actuality its inhabitant – the Vivienne of French Arthurian romance – hides within the dark forest of Broceliande because of her own fear of being misused, as the poem's end makes clear. Modern Vivienne locks herself so securely in her own defence mechanisms that she no longer feels like a woman.

'At the Abbey of St. Gildas de Rhuys' emerged when I visited the village square facing the church of St. Gildas, at the abbey to which Abelard was sent as abbot after the discovery of his seduction of Heloise and subsequent castration. A tourist sipping coffee sees a village woman flirting with a baker and suddenly regrets her own past as an academic who – like secluded monks – has spent too much time with books. The poem switches back and forth between the medieval setting with its envisioned past and the tourist who questions her own life choices. Intermingled with the scene are her feelings of envy of the village woman and her *Schadenfreude* over what she imagines might be the reality of the woman's situation – not unlike the envy mixed with irritation the monks must have felt about arrogant Abelard's fallen situation. She comforts herself by visualizing the village woman's husband as a drunk and her children as unloving, achieving a moment of empathy when that woman turns and the speaker realizes she is old, like her. What ends as barely penitential for Abelard – he actually returns to Paris – is perhaps equally self-delusion for the tourist: having made this literary pilgrimage to his abbey, she will retreat to her academic life when she leaves. And yet, "The Night the Books Fell," a poem that relays how a wall of medieval books cascaded down from their shelves during a thunderous storm during a scholar's vacation, suggests an imminent and symbolic change in her focus.

Other poems draw from images found in medieval art or in medieval or Renaissance works of literature. The ekphrastic 'Unicorn' reimagines a medieval past as expressed in art, satirising the artifice of the idea that all exists for aristocrats' own pleasure, as if a fantastic unicorn might attest to a queen's chastity. In this sense, the poem functions as humorous criticism of both class and period. *What might such a unicorn be thinking?* I ask, projecting myself into the pathetic beast locked within his garden and chained to a tree. In answer, I imagine he would want to be free to indulge his own sensuous and sensual animal pleasures, the contrast between the modern real and medieval fantastic ontology highlighting the hubris of medieval aristocracy.

Reinventing the Old English *Judith* in another poem involves identification with a male speaker, who becomes a modern Holofernes being decapitated/castrated, if you will, by a modern Judith who appropriates his 'sword' (masculine gender role). Invoking the symbolism of the Old English text, the poem emphasizes the anxiety of the modern male in the face of shifting norms for gender behaviour. Such fear of a strong woman, the poem suggests, often arises out of a man's sense of his own inadequacy, sexual or personal. Hence the title, 'The Savior of Worm Hall' – an allusion to the kenning of 'Worm Hall' as a metaphor for the grave – refers ironically to the bed in which the male persona imprisons himself, unable to act, in contrast to the symbol of the Anglo-Saxon warrior's joyous mead hall. In *Judith,* the saviour is not Christ, *salvatrix* for humankind, but captured hero Judith, leader of the Israelites, who decapitates drunken Holofernes when he presumes to seduce her. The only saviour for the persona of my poem is, of course, himself.

Other poems invoke the Middle Ages through a single image, as in 'Migration,' with its comparison of the sense of communal belonging experienced when entering a Gothic cathedral to the cyclical migration of wildebeests from Kenya to Tanzania, and in 'Humors for Ash-Wednesday,' with humors psychology used to chart changes in a love relationship.

Jane Chance

Aventure

The knight, newly dubbed, sets out one day,
his armor clattering as he heaves from block
to saddle, his long-maned stallion snorting
and stamping in early dawn-glimmer.
Does he first map out where might be giants?
And has he smarted and diced flesh
at all with that Toledo steel he wields?

Imagine a Sir Guyon wearying
of his father's complaint,
When will you slay your first dragon?
On his first quest, the heavy responsibility
of fronting the fire-breather,
his squire's service finished. For now
the chevalier can forget the smug-faced
older brother who sleeps while waiting
to inherit the castle.

And about that mission to fetch the abducted maiden -
maybe she isn't a maiden.
Maybe she is the grey-eyed girl he met
one summer as a page at knight camp at Suscinio
whose father might set
the right dowry-price after all.

But surely today what impels him
is simply the scent of meadow,
the huffing of steed, the heft
of a fine sword against plated thigh,
the sun bursting on the horizon
like a promise
in the long summer of his youth,
all whispering,
Go, see, try.

The Château de Comper

I am protected.
My drawbridge is double:
one bridge fixed over the moat
and another closer to me,
one that lifts. My arms are
locked above the gate, gaffs
grand in pose. I doubt
all softness,
all entreaty,

I refuse to negotiate terms.
Machicolation keeps me safe,
along with the beauty of distance.
The *chemin de ronde* behind
my battlements shows me proud,
if alone, sentried by the Giant
named I-Will-Never-Forget.

I have in fact been destroyed
several times, my careful stones
borne away for rebuilding stronger
by tanned arms.
So you who fancy you might enter,
you with the black hair and sweet face,
you who boast in metal,
know this: I am Vivienne,
I am the Château de Comper
bordered by Broceliande.

At moments, behind my dark mirrors,
I weep quietly so no one hears,
awaiting rescue.
Crenolated. Severe.
A castle imaginary.
A lady who has ceased to exist.

Jane Chance

At the Breton Abbey of Saint-Gildas de Rhuys

'The country was wild and the language unknown to me, the
natives were brutal and barbarous, the monks were beyond
control and led a dissolute life which was well known to all.'
Peter Abelard, *Historia calamitatum* (History of My Calamities)

Across from the abbey church, sipping coffee,
I spot a laughing woman buying bread.
Her waist-long blond hair furls in the sea-breeze,
her blouse is ruffled, green, with red roses,
her peasant skirt fringed in lavender.
Shaking her bracelets as she shifts
her sandaled feet, she reaches over
to touch the baker's hand.

I wish I had been her, not always hunched
over books, like Abelard, master of *Yes and No*,
sought out by students of so many tongues,
who locked his tongue with that of his host's niece.
Shorn of a future – their son, Astrolabe, aside –
an abbot in exile at the abbey, soon poisoned.
I think: monkish Schadenfreude.
The abbey church sits in stone silence.

I imagine her husband at home in bed
cuddling his empty bottle
of Côtes du Rhone. Likely her children
are brutal and say they don't love her,
this moment the bright purchase of her day.
For a second she turns toward me,
her lined face as worn as fine leather
left to rain, and the baker, the man
she loved as a girl.

Like Abelard fleeing to Paris
to live greater lies, I rise,
shedding books as I go,
the cold ochre stones of the church
a text for the blind: no longer
a lesson in humility
but in masking.

Still, she wears her joy as costume,
her regrets, as jewelry.

Jane Chance

The Night the Books Fell

The night the shelves shuddered off the wall
after twenty-three years of bolstering books
in a noise not unlike that of the end of the world–
from a book's point of view, as indeed it was–
when the dowels and brackets gave way,
in that moment when the old historical house
shook and trembled, cracked by thunderstorms
in the middle of dreams, it must have thought
(if thought it could have), At last!

The books hailing down in sheetrock dust
reached as far as the front door, the floor
rushing up to meet them, spines cracked,
Sir Gawain's back entirely broken,
and the Hobbit's; Virgil's and
Dante's covers torn and ripped,
and the others, piling one atop another, lost in the
tumult, as if they, too, just wore out.

Why this one storm after so many?
The tough edge of discipline
slackened, next to the need to give way.
A nervous breakdown of knowledge
gone astray. Atlas weary of lifting
the earth from the ground,
just to keep his strength, but then
that sheer rush of relief at letting go and
it doesn't matter anymore,
as if dropping off the edge of the earth.

Somewhere else in France, the professor
who owned them awoke suddenly,
and then, remembering where she was,
felt glad once more to be retired
after years of research and teaching, not yet knowing
about the fall of the books, as if,
by means of this cosmic sign
relieved of the obligation
of learnedness
and granted the divine gift of
pleasure in being
simply
human.

Jane Chance

Unicorn

The unicorn in the tapestry,
encircled by a burnished fence,
smiles despite the chain on his neck,
bound tight to the tree.
His tail curls into bouquets,
his image framed by a winding trellis
of green leaves and golden flowers.
From heaven, white blossoms plummet -
daisies, lilies, Queen Ann's lace.

The tree that tethers him multiplies
ruby pomegranates cradled by leafy boughs.
The letters A and E marry
at the end of the braid that girdles
the slim middle of its trunk.
He no longer awaits a virgin
into whose lap he must lay his head
to be caught. His mission fulfilled,
he is of course happy,

for Anne is surely a beautiful virgin
whose future husband is probably rich.
Like the tree, they will be fruitful and multiply.
Her unicorn, tapestry-captive, attests
to her perfection and purity,
sign and symbol of success.
But what is the unicorn thinking, do you suppose?
He is looking up, his horn very stiff,
his little eye upturned to Anne's boudoir ceiling,

plain tuckered out from this fantasy,
just wanting oats and alfalfa cubes,
as if he were not imaginary
and tired of being symbolic.

Jane Chance   26

He'd like to sleep a little, or play with others,
leave town and get a little dirty,
have a cool drink, find a girl,
let down his horn.

*The Unicorn in Captivity, seventh in the Hunt for the Unicorn
Tapestries (1495-1505, South Netherlandish, Metropolitan Cloisters,
New York), commissioned by Anne of Brittany for her marriage to
Charles VIII of France.*

The Savior of Worm Hall

Then the one with braided hair struck
the enemy with her adorned sword,
struck the hostile-minded one so that she cut through
half of his neck—so that he lay in a swoon,
drunk and wounded.—The Old English Judith

The sun shivers through smudged panes
while shadows twist to surface. Cyclists
wheel enormous bikes below,
freely dwarfing trees to blades.
Dumb and deaf, I
sit, pierced by stillness.

Picasso's print of the woman's face snakes
in red and black. Such a woman walls my
life. More ice – to warm with gin. But moving – my
feet have frozen, so motionless, in these snow sheets.
Frozen to the heart, wrapped in darkness,
surrounded by worms. Streets have
diminished, in driving, the route to this
bed. When this old body numbed, its
sex melted. So I sleep, and
the street outside will be lit with rain. Seeing
her – to remember – not just the daggering fingers,
the curling of talons like blackbirds' after death.
(These on my throat. Her proper prey. She smells my guilt.)
The woman mirrors me, her familiar bars and
restaurants, her intimate office, even her singular
street, all. All alone
the spirit journeys elsewhere – under steep cliffs –
yet to drive, one foot light
on accelerator – ah, and
motion, movement

past tight pink
landscapes. Maybe to Mexico. No, there is
no place.

More gin, the glass is empty –

to dwell in this worm hall forever
the dark home deprived of joy -

On the dark side of the Moon
walled creatures erect black houses
shutting off grace.

Hammering, hammering.
Such perverse fingers nailing
hands and feet.

I sit, crucified to stillness.

Migration

Cloven hooves of an ox, back legs of a horse,
mane of a lion, face of the *ngiri*, the warthog.
The wildebeest, Kenyans laugh, *so ugly*
only a mother could love him, migrates
in dark herds across the Mara like a wave,

moving south to the Serengeti and back again to Kenya.
The sun filtering through his golden mane
as he lopes along in his uneven way
suddenly seems just right, a different kind of balance,

like light through stained glass in a chill Gothic cathedral
that draws you in – the surprise, once past massive carved doors
into heavy darkness, only then seeing you're not alone,
but one of many, you and the wildebeests

in endless repetition, season in and season out,
natural music in time, in time.

Humors for Ash-Wednesday

Last night, rich in drink, I tasted
loving's dark constraint. Oh, I endured
the melancholic humor. I lifted the glass high

to finish grief. The juice gambled
my veins, winning current,
teaching me how to generate.

I once saw fruit displayed – inspired, guessed
black grapes would age to wine -
not flowers, destined to crackle simply and die.

Or so I thought. Back then,
I had lemon in my style of space.
I still would savor yellow over black,

humoring choleric realities.
But fire would bake my clay into a brittle hero,
hardening love. I'll drink again tonight.

Jane Chance

Pam Clements

I have been a Professor of medieval English language and literature for at least thirty years. I have written poetry for much longer. Having been immersed in the works of Chaucer, the author of *Sir Gawain* and *Pearl*, and the Anglo-Saxon poets, as well as in the long Arthurian tradition, it stands to reason that my poetry is affected by this lifelong immersion in medieval ideas, themes, and language. It is no surprise, then, that even in the poems that have no direct, or even indirect, connection to the medieval, I find myself using vocabulary tinged with medievalism.

My poetry, with a few exceptions, falls into the category of contemporary lyric, involving closely observed commentary on the natural and human-made world. The poems I've selected for this anthology are in addition imbued with the medieval, in ways varying from overt to oblique. Some of them describe medieval objects or beings that have long fascinated me. Of the poems included in this anthology, 'Wodewose' imagines the well-known figure of the Wild Man of the Woods as an embodiment of the life force, or more specifically, of vegetation. I have moved him – or spread his territory – to North America, where he is 'lord of kudzu.' 'Vivien/Merlin' directly references Merlin's imprisonment, here in an oak tree, but moves the legend into the industrial or postindustrial world. And 'Misericord' meditates on a particularly medieval object with regard to its uses both physical and philosophical.

Moving a bit farther from the literal, in 'Silkie' I reinterpret the old legend of the seal people, which may or may not stretch back into medieval times, placing it on today's Atlantic beaches, on some of which you might see seals playing. Writing 'Foxgloves at Glendalough' allowed me to imagine the lives of the monks who inhabited those Celtic ruins. 'White Owl Irruption' focuses on a more recent phenomenon, addressing the movement of large numbers of Snowy Owls into the northeastern United

States from their arctic homes. Thinking of them as Vikings in bird form called me to try to evoke them with a version of the Anglo-Saxon alliterative line.

The last two poems are informed by medieval images, and one might say *moods*, although they are clearly otherwise contemporary. 'Anhaga' takes its title from 'The Wanderer'; although its speaker is a (US) northerner living in the old Confederate South, the sense of being *essentially* lonely, without shoulder-companions who share an understanding of the world, is elegiac in the same sense as the Old English poem. 'Death, with a Discus' is an ekphrastic poem based on a self-portrait by Stephen Hannock, titled *Man of Peace, Child of the Nuclear Age*. He paints himself dressed for working with luminous paints, which he did for a time; he is wearing a long apron and a helmet, and carries his palette and a handful of paintings almost as a shield. He is surrounded by a set of exotic studio objects, and the atmosphere is mysterious, dark. My mind, as it does so often, went directly to the medieval, and 'Man of Peace' and 'Nuclear Age' conflated to a weird sort of artistic and ironic knighthood. The language of that poem glances off the medieval, and I hope, also does justice to the original painting.

Selecting eight poems for this collection showed me how much my poetic life is informed by my day job of teaching medieval literature. Many thanks to Oz for fostering group readings and now for assembling this anthology. It is wonderful to witness how much our critical, scholarly lives intersect with our creative lives. Medievalism is very much recognized as an important part of the 20th and now the 21st century cultural milieu; for the last few decades, critics have been fruitfully analyzing the impact of medievalism in fiction, drama, film, television, and videogames. It is time to add poetry to the world of contemporary medievalism.

Wodewose

A trail well marked
through second-growth forest,
lean sassafrass trees flirt/flash yellow mittens,
loam sponges underfoot
with moist smell
of death recycling.
Off trail, old oaks hung with cabled vines
lumped with shelf fungus: something winks.
Hint of a smile
where the green man resides
lies abundance

Wodewose, wild man of the woods
runs mad with his beard of moss;
whatever he touches, grows:
star moss, dogtooth violets, partridge berry,
Indian pipes spring from his step.
Just a pair of eyes a glint in ivy
vanishing.

Hildegarde called it *veriditas*
greening, freshening
spiritual fecundity, union with nature
by which she meant *the cosmos*, everything
living and dying beneath eyes of the woods;
stump turns to loam, leaf-mold to mushroom food.

The green man
plumps, dampens, makes seedpods burst
dirt in his fingernails, grit
in the creases of his hewn face.
He is Lord of Kudzu
and Dandelion,
of crabgrass, kelp cities,

wild grapevines, honeysuckle tangling the fences,
of lichens clasped to arctic rock,
the twinkle
of plenitude.

Foxgloves at Glendaloch

Instantly, you know
why Kevin chose this valley
for his meditation, why
those old saints
settled here
to build their tiny churches
and later, their round tower.

Tourists dissolve;
silence absorbs them.
Not quite silence, insect buzz
distills the afternoon.

Light through a mist
beyond the trail
that leads to Kevin's Cave
the ledge where he could lie
breathing over water, lightness, air
(only a saint
can sleep on slate
and wake to glory).

Seven roofless
weed-cornered
unruly chapels
the size of modern hotel rooms
are linked by grass, by headstones
by crosses carved,
the pencil-shape, the height
of tower.

Away from the ruins,
away from gift shops,
snapping cameras,

Pam Clements   36

girls embracing the high cross
to see who's next to marry,
you walk the path along the water,
a river of foxgloves
nodding, lush as chorus girls,
pallid, freckle-tongued, deadly,
dappling the wood's floor,
waking the ruins
in humus-rich recognition
of life everlasting.

Pam Clements

Death, with a Discus

After Steven Hannock's painting, **Man of Peace, Child of Nuclear Age**

Knight of a chemical era:
a single figure, armored,
aproned, robed in corduroy –
perhaps a cellarer
or castellan.

Where is this dark studio,
this airless basement room
tucked beyond moat and portcullis?
Its brick walls contain exotica from Samarkand
and just below deep ceiling beams,
a ropy-muscled Christ looks on.

Balancing a rounded object
(palette, frisbee, paten, Grail?)
on careful fingertips –
visible hand bandaged, or is that a latex glove?
one finger missing

Too-large helmet-head emerging
radioactive, taped and tinfoiled
eyeless, glowing, grimacing,
spattered with – with something;
a trinity of arrows clutched point-down

Beyond, in darkness
a peacock feather,
an open door
things damaged, things
unfinished.

Silkie

Once the bathing suit is left on shore
once afloat
bodies round, sleeken
shapes simplify
buoy
slick sleek
glide past weirs
anchorholds of lobster pots
kelp ruffles and bladders,
the only verticals
an element apart.

Oh to grow gills
fluted as coffee filters
transparent inner lids
to focus sight
through salt water
to mussel, limpet, barnacle
grips on rocks.

One dolphin kick
slides past humanity
fat becomes warmth
movement labile;
play is a swirl
with others roiling
then to flop on sand
barking with my kin
who loll on sandbars
flank to flank
in noisy caucus.

Pam Clements

Salt dries taut on weary bodies,
orange-billed terns streak overhead,
boats float the channel, jammed
with human observers
keeping respectful distance
amazed as our round heads
appear in the water
amazed at the gaze
of our large intelligent
liquid, long-lashed
Silkie eyes.

Vivien/Merlin

Maybe I wake up
under an oak tree
roped close with vines,
moss bound,
in warm air heavy,
fringed with honeysuckle,
delicate, greedy, drenching the air
with desire.
Maybe I've been imprisoned
for ages, centuries,
in this sharp bark.

Maybe it is twilight
when I first awake, and the nightjars
are piercing the air like pine
through wisteria,
weeds curling questions
at the root of this tree.
Maybe the owls are calling
and perhaps I understand them.
Maybe I remember
that I was friends with the birds,
that I swept away moss
like a housewife of wind;
maybe I know where roots tangle
underground, listening.

Or maybe I wake on a freeway
yawning to London's
bent metal citadels.
Maybe when I wake up rushing
no one will be there
to give magic meaning.

Pam Clements

White Owl Irruption

First they came flying,   fast as Finn at Finnsburgh
when he lay swift sword   in steady lord's lap
looking for raw revenge.   So did these raptors
beat on, wind-rowing,   catching breezes, breath or blow,
steadily southward,   stealing by night
down from the tundra,   tacking against time.
Snow-backed owls, ominous,   oaring toward food,
sustinence needed, in search of prey,   presently pensive,
late-lighting on rooftops,   landing in marshes
hungry, hollow,   come to harbor here,
virtual Vikings   invading our shores,
baring barred backs   to bask in winter sun.

Anhaga

A waterfall of loss,
reading Anglo-Saxon elegies;
singed catalpa leaves
drop in warm rain.
Adrift in this soft country,
a pit of longing gulfs
the ache of steel and snow,
for muffled clothing.
Palmettos clap thin plats
where wind should keen and wail
that anyone so loved should have the gall to die.

Here, they go bare-legged in November
in fleshy-bosomed air
Anhanga, eardstapa –
it might be any season.
The drifter steps across a sandy pale,
longing and anger
in-wound together.
Friends leave, loves fail.
Eala beorht bune.

Where are the beasts of battle?
Where are sleet's elf-arrows?
Where the fire-dim hall?
This winter-warmth admits to no conclusions.
In softness, grieving drowns.
Ache arches my bone-home.

Pam Clements

Misericord

The leering face
beneath one's seat
sticks out its tongue,
puffs cheeks like Boreas on ancient maps.
Polished weekly by the sexton,
russet cheekbones
burnished along grain
monkeys crouch in corners,
lovers feel each other up,
a friar shows his backside.

This underworld
contradicts the priest
homily and censer;
it's the snicker in the pews
when someone farts,
the gargoyle on the roof
with carnival gestures.
Some humble carver
made these things,
pleased to imagine
the pious perched
atop grotesqueries.

Oz Hardwick

I am an artist by nature, an academic by accident. I have
written – mainly poetry – for most of my life, have a spell at art
school tucked away in my dim and distant past, am engaged in
an ongoing struggle with a number of stringed instruments, and
regularly publish, perform, record, and generally create in
whatever medium feels right at the time. Somewhere along the
line, after reaching what seemed to be stalemate in my creative
development, I decided to enrol for an English and History of
Art degree in York. The course certainly led my life in an
unexpected direction – the only serious career decision I had
ever made being that I *most definitely* didn't want to teach – and
revisiting medieval literature for the first time since an
inauspicious encounter with Chaucer in high school was one of
my life's rare epiphanies. An equally important influence,
however, was the city itself, in which I still live.

York is one of those fortunate cities which, in these straitened
times, still remains buoyant. It faces the challenges of the 21st
century, however, by looking to its past, which it both
consciously and unconsciously represents and recreates.
Medieval churches remain in use, while modern shop fronts give
way to historic interiors, streets mark ways that have been
walked by Romans and Vikings, and medieval survivals,
pastiches and re-enactments are all part of daily life.
Consequently, it is a city which seems to exist between times, so
while it is a flourishing, often crowded city, it is also a
temporally liminal imaginative space. As such, it is a city which
elicits a profound affective response within me: a response that
has been the generative impulse for most – if not all – of my
work of the past 25 years, whether directly or indirectly.

I have always been attracted to the margins, whether that has
meant photographing oppositional musical subcultures in the
80s, or crawling around church floors researching my
monograph on misericords. These are the spaces of fluidity, the

conceptual borderlands through which one passes between states – chaos to order, profane to sacred and, indeed, past to future – where, however firmly inscribed the physical signs may be, mutability is the only constant. My work as an academic explores these spaces, and their shifting boundaries, interrogating the ways in which they comment upon, magnify, reflect, complement, subvert, distort or restate dominant cultural narratives. My work as an artist, in whatever medium, does exactly the same, and I find the European Middle Ages – and its material survivals through which I pass on a daily basis – an inexhaustible source of stimulus for both.

In a 2000 article on Alan Garner's *The Owl Service*,[7] I suggested that popular notions of the Middle Ages as a time of irrationalism and disorder act within the novel as a metaphor for adolescence. As someone with bipolar disorder, I am acutely aware that the aspects of the medieval which fascinate me, as I have sketched briefly above, make for an equally apt metaphor for the way I experience the world, occupying a constantly shifting point between two states. All of which makes it seem pretty much inevitable that I should find myself in, fittingly, middle age, in a city caught between past and present, studying and responding to the margins of a period, the precise limits of which are contested.

For all their diversity, and frequent polar oppositions, these fragments – physical, temporal, intellectual, aesthetic and psychological – cohere for me into an indivisible yet constantly self-refashioning whole: how I think, what I do and, ultimately, who I am. Like most art, in any medium and on any scale, my poetry represents part of my attempt to make sense of this whole, and to articulate this inevitably partial understanding in a manner that may perhaps connect in a meaningful way with a hoped-for reader. To this end, I find that employing medieval forms, tropes and images, gathered serendipitously and

---

[7] '"Not in the Middle Ages"?: Alan Garner's *The Owl Service* and the Literature of Adolescence,' *Children's Literature in Education* 31.1 (March 2000), 23-30.

peremptorily marshalled to my particular needs of the moment, offers me a language with which I can begin to touch upon my concerns.

Whether it is in the ekphrastic meditation upon the beasts that occupy the margins of medieval art, the interweaving of apocalyptic prophecy with current news reports, or the metamorphosis of silent voices, these poems argue that we are always residing in the Middle Ages, experiencing both its reassuring familiarity and *unheimlich* otherness. If, as both Anglo-Saxon elegy and TV talent shows constantly remind us, life is a journey, we must, like the Exeter Book's *Seafarer*, choose our mode of travel and the nature of that journey. Poems are often found on the most storm-battered shores: these are some that I have gleaned from voyages through the 'Middle Ages.'

Funeral at Walcourt

Tuesday lunchtime: Saint-Materne is closed
for a funeral, the muted murmur of music
accompanying the *chink* of three-handled glasses
as we sample the local beer, and wait.

Inside, there will be sadness, probably tears
but, I like to think, some celebration
of life lived long and well. But
that isn't why we are here. I wonder,

are family, friends, casual acquaintances,
thinking of what hides beneath the stalls-
giants, goats and grimacers, naked women
mounting naked men, a preaching fox,

a congregation of gullible geese,
a wimpled virago leading her victim
by his bound bollocks, straining squatters
shitting on mermaids' mirrors? Maybe

or maybe not. Five centuries on,
these raucous guests have still not learnt
to behave, their sexy, satiric, scatological
antics a most indecorous decoration.

The church door swings open, darkness
disgorging mourners into the Belgian afternoon
as we finish our drinks. There's chatter on the pavement,
someone lights a fag as the coffin emerges

shaky into sunshine, awkwardly manhandled
into the back of a battered estate, its protruding end
clumsily bungeed to the loose bumper before
the engine splutters and they bounce away.

Inside the hushed choir, someone farts.

The Green Man Awakes

Dreaming myself awake, my mouth,
flower-full, overflows with fragrance,
overpowers you, kisses spring
into lithe limbs waking from winter.

Mine is the voice of the virile vine,
the twisting tongue that tempts and teases,
tangles your senses, sets your mind
rushing, racing, dancing, spinning

till I catch your thoughts in knot and grain,
in leaf and line, snaking stems
and the sensuous seduction of breathless scents,
surging and scintillating. But mine is the dark

green of the holly bough; handsome, unflinching,
bearing fortune and truth, strength and tears,
the sharp cure, each leaf a door
opening, closing: dare you pass through?

And in my green twining, I offer you
rubies, blood-red at ankle and finger,
plumped fruit juicing parted lips,
and the skipped beat of a waking heart.

Oz Hardwick

The Green Man Sleeps

Long-dead fingers gouged my eyes
closed, cleft my web-wound tongue
into tubers, spewing leaves from splinters.

My sallow face, hinged into shadow,
is intimate with darkness, my barren buds,
a court of worms. Lift me up,

listen to my tale of time, slow
motion, and understand I am still
breathing.

Annunciation

Silence. The dark of extinguished stars
shadows all senses, doubt
clouds numbed voices. The weight
of words unwritten drowns thought
beneath the stubborn rush of nothing.

And I pray: not for the voice, not
for the touch, taste, sight, smell
or sound, but for the sharp annunciation
of fire, the heart's bright kindling,
the understanding beyond understanding.

Journey to the West
From the Old Norse **Vestrfaravísur**

Ship of speech, word-wave,
sails westward, and I, speaking,
hold hard to wind's unfolding
across air's parchment, writing.

Lords and lackeys murmur and mill
and I, outside, stoop and supplicate,
seek king's councillors, crave
access and audience, a prince who pays
for tongue's treasure, mind's unfolding,
richly wrapped in iron rings.

Earls of earth's serpent spend
safety, scorn stability, senses
stripped; proud proclaimers, power-drunk,
cast kings' cares to the wind's casket.
Let warriors wait hard on heath;
hope under heaven favours flight.

Broad battles rage bitter,
brave lords drain heart's mead,
unstinting drink the wine of ravens,
speak soft words, plough hard rows.

Mine is the gift of gold, speaking
strong lines; yours is steel,
a sharp sword, a worthy weapon.
A wise warrior weighs God's words.

Wind's servant, across the shifting hills
I return, richer in words and welcomes,
giving gifts undiminishing, gaining
grace of place, proud amongst peers.

Oz Hardwick

I have fared far, fought clinging coils
of earth's duplicitous dragon, found
home, the giver of true gifts:
one word resolves all riddles.

True Thomas

When hares whelp on hearthstones and whales swim in the City,
Wit and Will shall war together.
Then a barrel of oil shall cost a barrel of blood
as man leads man in chains to market.

When fathers are forgotten and sons prove false,
Pride will preen and Peace be imprisoned.
Then a madman will be monarch through his own misdeeds
as hunger harries more than half the world.

When a lamb with six limbs lurches and falls,
fruits shall fail through flood and foul weather.
Then waves will wax wild while women thirst,
as a false sun smiles and seals our doom.

When shall this be? It is sadly seen:
In your time and mine and the time between.

Oz Hardwick

Merlin's Tree

Black rot bear me, apple tree:
wait in vain for fruit. Wars sound,
rake roots, tremble barren earth,
crack lands. In summer, leaves spread
shade, but winter bites, storms' teeth
gnaw bark, eat dark days, spit bones

unfit for crows. Boughs bend,
blister, break. Cold frog eye
leaf spot spreads. Scores of years
slung beneath impatient sky,
surveying battles; dead life
lived with wild ones in the wild.

Speak, pig: what news of one
who was so fair? Icicles answer,
pierce thin skin, burn bright
fire blight. Mars rises red,
writes ruin: cork spot,
crown rot, apple scab.

The Seafarer's Return

My salt-caked sea chest is heavy with shells and stones
gathered from empty beaches. *Rough Guides*
never mention such places: dangerous tides
deter all but the most determined. I have travelled alone,
gleaning beauty from shores where seas had thrown
silence upon silence upon silence, where forever hides
in the glimmer of spray, where no gull glides
on dead air and secrets remain unknown.

At your door I stand, tongue tied in weed,
footsore, with blistered palms and a distant stare,
my shoulders stooped with the weight of my journey. I need
more than I can ask. But first, share
these far-gathered gifts of shell and stone
whose value resides in the grace of you alone.

M. Wendy Hennequin

I am a poet. I am also a scholar of medieval literature. Strangely enough, these aspects of my life developed simultaneously. I wrote my first poems for undergraduate courses and my first attempts at Old English poetry as I was finishing my Masters. Both the scholar and the poet in me are fascinated by medieval literature and poetic forms. To the scholar, medieval works are puzzles to be analyzed, their meanings to be sought like treasure. To the poet, medieval texts are already treasures, masterpieces of form, design, and beauty that equally inspire creativity and jealousy. When my scholar and poet work together, however, they both benefit: the poet uses the scholar's knowledge to understand, imitate, and add to form and content, and the scholar gains a more visceral understanding of how and why the form and content worked – and still work.

If I was called to be a poet, the call came in an unusual form: extra credit for writing sonnets in an undergraduate class. I did not really begin writing medieval poetry consistently until a few years later. Then my inspiration came partially from the love of the literature, but more from my friends and colleagues. Many, like me, fell in love with the Middle Ages as children. Some, like me, have entered academia, and others study the Middle Ages as a hobby. Several of these medievally-minded friends, I discovered, wrote and exchanged medieval style poetry and poetry on medieval subjects. So I decided that I, too, would write medieval poetry – not from fondness for the forms, or a Romantic nostalgia for the past, or even a poetic vocation, but to impress my friends. Later, this desire to impress migrated with me to graduate school, where I wrote a poetic translation of *Judith* and Old English style riddles to impress my professors. And, yes, it worked. But whether I wrote for my professors or my friends, the same pattern emerged: what I studied in medieval literature inevitably made its way into my poetry.

The poet and the scholar in me are as hopelessly entangled as the lines of Celtic knotwork. The poet in me might think a piece beautiful and inspirational. The scholar takes the poet's idea and wonders about poetics, plot evolution, and other possible re-incarnations of story, themes, and forms. 'Guðrinc's Lament,' included here, serves as a case in point. I discovered that a friend had studied Classics and was particularly fond of *The Iliad*. I was working with Old English at that time and offered to write an Old English-style poem for him based on an episode of *The Iliad*. As this friend also studied martial arts, I expected a request for the death of Hector or Patroklos, and prepared myself to write an epic. My friend requested instead a poem about Hector and Andromache on the walls of Troy. I as poet began to think about the episode and look for inspiration, emotional and plot approaches; I as scholar began to tackle the poem as a problem. How would the Anglo-Saxons view this domestic episode? Perhaps my poet decided that the tale of Andromache had to be an elegy, but my scholar knew why and looked to Old English elegies for ways to approach and integrate the classical material into an Anglo-Saxon mindset. The poet thought that making Andromache an Amazon would be cool.[8] The scholar justified the decision by the meaning of the name Andromache (something like 'battle of men' in Greek) and the Anglo-Saxon use of kennings. Scholarly knowledge and poetic sensibilities wove together a retrospective story of loss, defeat, and exile, consciously attempting to be an Old English elegy.

As a poet, my two particular interests in medieval poetry are the poetics and the tradition of retelling and building on previous stories. I have always loved medieval poetic forms. Chaucer's musical river of flowing verse, the gentle lilting of *Sir Gawain*'s bob and wheel, and the powerful drumbeat of stress and alliteration in *Beowulf* all sing to me from the page and resonate in my soul. I also have a hard time, both as poet and scholar, understanding the poetics of free verse, but medieval

---

[8] Marion Zimmer Bradley's *Firebrand* may also have influenced me, though I cannot remember if I read *Firebrand* before or afterwards.

M. Wendy Hennequin

forms also have quantifiable and describable techniques, poetics with rules and patterns. When I began to write medieval poetry, I naturally turned to these forms, forms that I love and understand and can emulate. The scholar understands how medieval poetics work; the poet internalizes them and makes them work for me and for my own stories.

My interest in the retelling and building of stories also grew out of my scholarship. The scholar in me has always been fascinated by how time, place, and authorial (and patronal) interest changes versions of the same story, and how new authors build on older works, adding plots and characters to an already established canon. This practice was commonplace in the Middle Ages: authors constantly worked, re-worked, and expanded the stories of Arthur, Charlemagne, Troy, saints, and even the Bible. This practice has never died – we now call it participatory or fan fiction. My fascination with such reworked stories began with the various characterizations of Sir Gawain, an interest which I still retain, and which has inspired no fewer than four of my poems. But as the scholar progressed, the poet found new 'universes' to work and play in, and new stories to tell and re-tell.

Like Guðrinc, I 'long for the days of dear-worthy joys / Shield and sword-fame, songs of the fight.' I cannot live in those days, nor, given social and physical realities of the Middle Ages, would I really want to. But as a scholar, I can study that time, read its poetry and history, learn its ideas and its stories. That knowledge allows me, as a poet, to think myself into those days and understand them in a way that the scholar cannot. My scholar attempts to understand the poems of the Middle Ages; my poet tries to sing with them.

Guðrinc's Lament

Once were these walls— well I remember—
Carved with serpents,   covered with gold,
Shining and splendid.   Steadfast and strong,
They bravely stood,   when the sea-riders,
Ship-warriors,   the shore invaded,
And conquered the sand.   Shining, they stood,
Bright guardians,   gated in glory,
Bearing warriors   in bright helmets,
Battle-brothers   brave among men,
Who first charged forth,   famous in war,
To fight with the foemen.   Fallen and broken,
Wounded in limbs,   they lie on the earth,
Proud guardians,   plundered for stone,
Carried away,   like carrion for beasts,
As high houses   and holy dwellings
For the out-landers,   old lie-crafters.
Where are you now,   walls of splendor,
Brilliant as dawn,   bravely shining,
When I came riding,   ready-hearted,
Eager for war,   and you welcomed me
With open gates?   Glory in battle
I came seeking,   sent by the queen,
Skilled in fighting.   Fleeting it was,
Ten winters long   of war-battle
Before the walls,   weary of the fight,
Fell to the earth   after the fierce struggle,
And lay, resting,   after the long battle.
There, the gold-giver   greeted me kindly
Beneath the wall-gate,   woven with gold,
And the sea-riders,   ship-warriors,
Mocked my coming.   Keenly they paid!
There did I stand   beside the shining wall,
Spear in my hand   for hard fighting,

Shoulder against shoulder   with the sword-warrior,
The man-killer,   mightiest prince,
And Man-Battle   my mother called me.
Well did they learn it!   The line-warriors
Fled before us,   fast to their ships,
Before the might   of the man-killer,
Mighty in war,   and Man-Battle.
That noble warrior,   wisest of princes,
Praised me for skill—   the ship-raiders
Plundered his bed-rest   for beaten gold.
Shield against shield,   they shattered the walls,
And I stood at the house   of the high maiden,
Holy dwelling,   and hefted my spear,
Shoulder against shoulder   with my small sister,
Seer of truth;   she a sword wielded.
She fought nobly!   Fallen that house,
But no foemen's hands,   foul defilers,
Sullied the maiden.   Smiling, she stood,
When the noble prince,   proud warrior,
Gave me a ring   of ruddy gold,
Ring-giver's gift   for glory in battle.
Against the ancient custom   of my kinswomen,
I, glad, received it.   Gone is that house,
The good dwelling.   Gone is the prince,
The man-killer,   mighty in war.
Gone is the mead-hall,   gleaming with gold,
Where the high-lord sat,   longing for war,
The noble youths,   yearning for battle.
The young fighters,   famous in war,
Fell by the wall-gates.   Folded in earth
Those kinsmen lie,   kinswomen too,
Noble war-women   in white armor,
Slain beside the walls.   I watched, weary,
From high towers,   as the heathen foe,
Dreaded shipmen,   shield against shield,
Fought on the shore,   shared their sword-blades.
Eager for battle,   babe in my arms,

I longed for my spear.   My sword-brother,
The man-killer,   mighty in war,
Famous in battle,   fated to die,
Circled me in arms,   spoke comfort to me.
I found joy in that—   fierce sorrow too.
And the child knew not   his noble father,
Nor noble mother;   many the tears.
Where is the warrior   who walked beside me,
Strong on the field,   fierce in battle,
The brave hero,   brilliant in helm?
Where the ring-giver,   ruler of the town?
Where are the princes,   the proud warriors?
The city-dwellers,   seeing no harm,
Opened the gates.   Gone the ring-giver,
The kinswomen,   and the warrior-queen!
Gone is the city,   shining as dawn!
Gone are the walls,   where I watched, maddened,
When fell the might   of the man-killer,
Skilled in the fight,   and the ship-warriors,
Foreign foemen,   defiled his flesh-home.
The walls shattered   before the sea-riders' might,
And they plundered the hall,   heavy with silver,
And plundered the tombs,   treasure-laden,
And raided the house   of the high maiden,
And slew all the warriors   and wise women,
Maidens and wives,   and many children,
And flames engulfed   the gold-city.
They freed me later,   fools that they are,
Spared me my son   and the seer of truth.
The ship-warriors   s ent from the city
My kinswomen,   keen in the fight.
We walk, exiles,   who once were rulers,
Queen and kinswomen,   keen warriors,
Long for the days   of dear-worthy joys,
Shield and sword-fame,   songs of the fight,
Feastings in hall,   and heart-friendships.
Oh, the man-killer,   mightiest prince!

M. Wendy Hennequin

Oh, the ring-giver,   ruler in hall!
Oh, worthy queen,   keen warriors,
Battle-companions,   brave in the fight,
Brothers and cousins,   keen kinswomen!
Oh, the bright city,   shining and splendid!
We wait by the walls.   Well I remember.

Hear you, Steel-Heart?   The song you began
And thought finished   when fell the walls
Of the radiant city   I, ready-hearted
Sing new verses,   noble in deeds
Weaving with words   a warrior's ending.
I shall end easily   what you, eager, began:
A battle song.

Three Old English Riddles

Feohteð cwene   fah beowulfes,
Spere felamodige   flitð cræftlice.
Ealdorwis   wiggend welig
Awendeð ealdcræfte   eorþan renan
In deorwyrðlicne gold,   gife cwene.

The bee-wolf's foeman   fights for the queen,
Spars skillfully   with spear valiant.
Wealthy war-thane,   wiser than ancients,
Alters with old craft   earth-adornments
To precious gold,   gift for the queen. [9]

I am a wondrous wight,   warrior of skill,
Hunter in hall   where heroes drink,
Fierce against foes.   Five knives I bear
In either hand.   Eager for war,
I lay waiting,   watching for foes,
By night and day,   never ceasing.
No hall-raider,   hard warrior,
Escapes my grip.   Grim life-reaver,
I devour his flesh,   feast on his blood.
But gentle I am,   guardian of the hall,
Hearth-companion   where heroes drink.
I lay my head   in the hall-maiden's lap.
She strokes my hair.   A soothing song
I sing by the hearth.   Say what I am.[10]

---

[9] Bee
[10] Cat

M. Wendy Hennequin

I am a wondrous wight,   weighty creature,
Wise beyond counsel.   I come often
In the high mead-hall   where heroes drink
And find a way   into the women's chambers,
Seeking secrets   in the side bowers.
My face, covered;   cloaked my body:
None but the wise   know me ever.
Single my eye,   and a serpent's tongue,
A hand mighty,   and a handsome key
That fits no lock.   I make madness
To trap men's souls.   Many seek me
To learn my secret.   Say what I am. [11]

---

[11] Riddle

The Bard's Tale

At Christmastide, good Arthur, England's king,
    At table sat with Guinivere, his Queen,
    And noble knights around him in a ring.
Then suddenly, within their midst was seen
    A lady in a gown of gold and green.
    "I hear it is your custom, ere you eat,
    To hear a story of a wondrous feat.

"So thus from Ireland did I take sail
    In this most joyous, deadly time of year,
    To bring before your grace myself and tale,
Which, please your grace, you presently shall hear."
    The king assented. "Nobles all, take ear
    And hearken to the tale for which I hied
    To Camelot. In February died

"My father good. In Ireland, no other
    In nobleness and sword-skill could compare.
He left no son, no nephew, nor no brother
    Behind him; thus my sister was the heir
    To crown and scepter and the land of Clare.
But swift and sudden came a fearsome band
    Of northern ravagers to steal our land.

"Their leader was a fierce and evil king,
And his six hundred knights that with him stayed
    Would force my sister wear his wedding ring.
Destruction, blood, and death in balance weighed,
    My sister gave assent. I sang and prayed,
    And on Saint Patrick's Eve, in driving rain,
    Came Bedivere and Kay and good Gawain.

     M. Wendy Hennequin

"A challenge to the northern king they sent,
For in the village, of our awful plight
Gawain had heard. 'Give over and repent,'
The northern king replied. ''Tis not your fight.'
'Not so! A lady to defend and right
Her wrong our privilege is,' said Sir Gawain.
'We came for justice; justly, we remain.'

"The northern king then offered land and gold.
'Take back your filthy offerings! We came
Not seeking rich rewards in metals cold,
Nor testing fortune, nor to prove our fame.
We came to help a lady, and you shame
Yourself with bribery,' said Sir Gawain.
'We came for justice; justly, we remain.'

"Six hundred knights had taken to the field
When dawn had broken on Saint Patrick's Day.
Three noble knights took vows to never yield
And charged. From battlements, I watched the fray.
How it was done, I cannot rightly say,
But on that field, six hundred knights were slain
By Bedivere and Kay and good Gawain.

"For this I came to Camelot today:
To tell this tale of wonder I have seen;
To thank Sir Bedivere, and good Sir Kay,
And Sir Gawain, who bears the baldric green,
As emissary of my sister, Queen
Of Clare. From Ireland, I thus took sail —
And so began, and endeth so, my tale."

"These words have come to Camelot newborn,"
Said Arthur King. "Why did you nothing say?"
"How should we speak?" cried Bedivere with scorn.
"'Twas just. There's nothing to be said." Sir Kay
Said nothing but, "Aye, just," and turned away.

Amazed, King Arthur turned to Sir Gawain.
"We went for justice. Thus did justice reign."

Ballade
for Carolyne la Pointe

When all the world in silent darkness lies
And all the daily work is at an end,
To rest and dreaming go the weary wise.
But I, instead, the tower stairs ascend;
And light my candles; quills and brushes mend.
From Compline bells, till Matins wake the night,
My hands in darkness work; my heart, in light.

My hand records the deeds of mighty kings,
The will of queens, their letters and decrees.
The sable ink upon the vellum sings,
A harmony of strokes. The eyes to ease
Of them who read, perhaps their hearts to please,
Is my desire and ever my delight.
My hands in darkness work; my heart, in light.

How glorious the colors, green and gold,
The black and scarlet, purple and the blue!
Though deep the night and bitter bites the cold,
And candles smoke, and colors shine untrue,
My dancing hands a woman's face imbue
With living truth of spirit and of sight.
My hands in darkness work; my heart, in light.

Envoi, to St. Katherine

O holy Katherine, of scribes the Queen,
Grant me thy grace, thy mercy, and thy might,
My hands to steady, heart and eyes make keen.
The scholar bless who did these verses write,
And let our works bring beauty and delight,
Though they may not attain the Heaven's height.
Our hands in darkness work; our hearts, in light.

Sonnet: Andromache Beside the Window Waits

Andromache beside the window waits
For Hector; Hector's gone this day to war
Against her dream, which prophecy he rates,
But go he must: the King he can't ignore.
Andromache beside the window waits.
Her little son is playing on the floor.
Too young to understand the clash of states,
He laughed farewell as Hector closed the door.
Andromache beside the window waits
Her husband—lover—whom she misses sore,
As news comes home with Troilus through the gates:
Achilles rides, and Hector is no more.
Soon all Troy rails against the gods and Fates.
Andromache beside the window waits.

M. Wendy Hennequin

A.J. Odasso

While my passion for writing poetry pre-dates my interest in / study of medieval English verse, my time spent pursuing the latter subject as both an undergraduate (2000 - 2005) and a graduate student (2005 - 2011) has noticeably influenced my work. I did not begin to submit poems for publication until late 2005, and it was by this point that the works of Chaucer, Langland, and the *Pearl*-Poet had strongly influenced my use of such devices as alliteration and kennings, as well as my tendency to write dream visions (*literal* ones). I'm a writer who spends a great deal of time examining what I can remember on waking, as the following selections demonstrate. Dreams are texts, and texts dreams; I'm unable to separate the act of writing from the act of dreaming. This, I feel, is the truest, most lasting legacy that these poets have left me.

Your last word on earth

might be my name, but it's hard to tell
through the prism of retraction. We sent

satellites forward in time at the speed
of thought; I need to know if I find you

again in the static, lest these glass bones
mis-refract. Message: *All that you love*

is enclosed in unforgiving stone. Response:
Then I will inter these shards, great city,

with your unrelenting ghost.

A.J. Odasso

Handle With Care

Needles, green. There's pine-sharp light
on this dove-feathered morning. Breeze
past rust-screened window, off leaves—

my mother's strayed, dawn-wise, roving
through bright trees. As for my father,
no-one knows where he sleeps. I shiver

to cousins' dismay. Witch-child, hellion,
so-young-she-speaks: *Where has mom gone?*
They marvel there's none so quiet as me

in my grief. *Orphaned early,* I think, but lack
enough breath to seethe. Word-wild, fearful,
slip cabin-latch and cinderblock. The breach

is old-wood, is shadow, is dust. Beyond it—
brave voices, bruised sea.

Brief History I

"You may see a cup of tea fall off of a table and break into pieces on the floor. But you will never see the cup gather itself back together and jump back on the table. The increase of disorder, or entropy, is what distinguishes the past from the future, giving a direction to time."
—Stephen Hawking, *A Brief History of Time*

*

Never mind, Doctor. The fact remains
the teacup shattered. I won't pretend
I didn't want to die; I won't pretend

I didn't want to *try*. There's what you
believe I am (strong); there's what
you believe and what it *is* (false).

The fact remains
the teacup shattered,
and my heart
lies scattered
on the floor.

Second Lives

Lost traces, last loves. These slip from me
like a fog. What dreams I can't recall, I leave
to the ages. You killed me. My blood froze
in its tracks for a time. Dead weight walking
is what I became, my every breath labored
as shrill winter air—and summer no better,
for when heat returned to my heart, it arrived
my vengeful ghost. Learn from terrors, know
that through anger we forge resurrection.

Winter Sun
after Chagall

Red angel, ring of gold. Midnight sun
is here now, and the needle's eye unfolds

into wholeness. Linger beneath blue-eyed pines
till morning, you frostbitten strangers. Stories told

are worth twice their weight in ruin. If you run
from the soaring arc of dawn, it will tell you

of snow that fell: a child's empty mitten,

her mother's grief a well.

Brief History II

Imagine my wonder
when the cup
began to mend.

Two fragments bent
this self-same rift
in time and space.

What My Mother Gave Me

My dream-self knows these twins I've borne
are impossible, remembers my restless body
rendered barren, recalls absence of wanting
for a child: so here are two, chestnut-haired
and bluet-eyed. *Flawless*, says my mother,

pulling firstborn, son, still slick and uncrying
from bloodless absence-of-womb. The second,
gazing widely at the room, arrives painless. I lift
the child to my shoulder, rise shaking, swiftly run
to the others in the kitchen—*Here is my daughter!*

What happens next isn't worth telling. My mother
wraps them, both living, for an ice-rimed grave.

(In this, in my dream,
I had no say.)

They will keep till we return, she explains.

Postscript (2012)

Surrendered: 12 months
to that dying. No dream
could draw me grasping

back to the sun. You claim
my mind shattered; I know
my soul took leave. Less

your love, less our history
amends have been made—
laid low in my grave. Won:

brass tacks for scar-lines,
prisms for eyes. Bury
remembrances bled,

still they do rise.

A.J. Odasso

Joe Martyn Ricke

As a medievalist, I'm drawn to the more exotic, erotic, far-out, bloody, grotesque, physical side of late medieval spirituality; for example, the devotion to the instruments of the passion of Christ or the prayers to the wounds of Christ make sense to me. For a little taste:

> Praise and honor be given Thee, O sweet and merciful Jesus, by reason of the Sacred Wound in Thy Left Foot. By this adorable wound, I beseech Thee to grant me pardon and full remission of all my sins, so that, with Thine aid, I may escape the rigors of justice. (attributed to Saint Claire of Assissi)

Or, more poetically put:

> Ihesus wounds so wide
> Ben welles of lif to the goode
> Namely the stronde of his syde
> That ran full breme on the rode.
> Yif thee liste to drinke
> To fle fro the fendes of helle,
> Bowe thou doun to the brinke
> And mekely taste of the welle
>   (from BM Ms Arundel 286, f.3)

I like late medieval apocalyptic stuff, loud stuff, outlandish stuff, fights between biblical patriarchs and their wives, shrewish saints, visions of the Virgin, crucified gods, the stigmata, Franciscan devotional practices, the lovely, grace-giving toes of the Virgin Mary on the statue that, as a child, I used to kneel before in Our Lady of Mercy Church in Mercedes, Texas, and the erotic body as the site of potential holiness. I wrote a dissertation about the late medieval versions of the Antichrist, but since then

have, for the most part, focused on late medieval drama –
writing about it, performing it, directing it, and recording it. I
like things dramatic, you could say. Maybe that stems from my
childhood realities and fantasies. My mother was a kind of all-or-
nothing convert to Catholicism with a strange mixture of
mysticism, poetry, depression, and self-dramatization. Growing
up Roman Catholic on the Texas/Mexican border, about a mile
from the Rio Grande River, I was part of a colorful, vibrant,
emotional, and dramatic religious culture, featuring coronations
of the Virgin in May, long, intense Good Friday services in early
spring, and, especially, the winter celebration of Nuestra Senora
de la Guadalupe, the subject of one of my poems in this volume.

I'm also a poet and a singer/songwriter, whose own creations
(and whose influences) might be characterized as edgy, parodic,
manic, risky, grotesque, witty, beat, baroque (if that includes
Donne, Crashaw, and the other so-called Metaphysical Poets),
and heavy on affect. My work features broken but beautiful
humans in a strange but possibly sacred place, full of doubts and
desires. I want people to dance, sing along, weep, 'walk' on their
knees from Roncesvalles to Santiago de Compostella, repent, get
angry at God, get right with God, give up on God, become a god,
fall in love with me, freak out, or memorize all my poems (better
yet, tattoo them across their bodies).

For some reason, I have mostly focused on women characters
in the early English drama, especially the so-called shrewish
wife. For the International Congress on Medieval Studies last
year, I organized and directed a series of performances (and a
discussion) of medieval plays which we titled 'Shrews before
Shakespeare.' Along the same lines, I have a chapter in the recent
MLA volume *Approaches to Teaching The Taming of the Shrew*
which attempts to provide a context for Shakespeare's play by
demonstrating the existence of a 'shrew play' tradition in the
Middle Ages.

Similarly, as a poet, especially as an ekphratic poet, I have been
drawn to depictions of women. I have written a number of what
I would call 'pure' ekphratic poems about specific works of art,
several of them medieval, such as the *Enthroned Virgin (Child*

Missing) in the Metropolitan Museum of Art in New York City, which is the subject of 'The Pricking of Divine Love' in this volume. I have other pieces which do the same thing with non-medieval works, like Paul Klee's depiction of Eve or Dali's Madonna. I have also written what I call 'mongrel' ekphratic poems, which, instead of interpreting a specific object, enter into dialogue with more of an artistic/cultural tradition or image (like the stigmata or the medieval fascination with representing Mary Magdalene as a beautiful prostitute with absurdly long hair). In this volume, I have a sequence of Mary Magdalene poems, as well as two which, in different ways, reflect on the Virgin Mary's own bloody wounds. One of those is a parodic (Kerouac-inspired) 'translation' of the beautiful and strange early 15th -century lyric, 'Adam Lay Ybounden,' in which the medieval author, like me, gives thanks for the fall and human sinfulness.

Last night I was reading Chaucer's *The Nun's Priest's Tale* to my sister, Missy, lightly transliterating as I went. Matching my own excitement in performance, she was overwhelmed with the copious over-determination, the wonderful excess of it all. It is not accident that she too, like me, loves the Beat writers, especially Jack Kerouac. I say this to apologize if my own work intentionally sprawls and over-reaches, even past the formatting requirements of this volume at times. So, if you wonder, dear reader, why the seven seven-line stanzas of Seven Sevens and an Envoy for Juan Diego sometimes leap past their prescribed (and announced) boundaries, please just do whatever you need to do to relax and not worry about it. In the divine economy which confronts me in my world of sense and imagination, one deity means three persons, one truth means four gospels, five wounds mean a world of hurt, and seven lines (not so much sloppy as slippery) mean the millions things we need to say before we can start to say anything at all.

Felix Culpa

Adam lay ibowndyn, bowndyn in a bond;
Fowre thousand wynter thowt he not to long.
And al was for an appil, an appil that he tok,
As clerkis fyndyn wretyn in here book.

Ne hade the appil take ben, the appil taken ben,
Ne hadde never our lady a ben hevene qwen.
Blyssid be the tyme that appil take was.
Therfore we mown syngyn, "Deo gracias."

(Anonymous, Early 15th Century)

Yeah, yeah, yeah, yeah, yeah.
Adam lay chained, the fucking heaviest chains you can imagine,
like something Blake would receive from an angel and then etch.
He'd been chained up so long I guess he'd even forgotten why.
A vague pain in his side, the absence of a complete skeleton,
reminded him of something he once knew or cared about.
Something about a pear, some rhubarb, some tasty dish he
    couldn't resist,
some love that, at the time, seemed more important than the
    alternatives,
some lesson he stood for, he symbolized, but it all seems long ago
    now.

Yet sometimes it turns out, and I'm not saying it always turns out
    this way,
that one man's fall is another man's (or woman's) grace,which is
    to say,
one man's woe is another man's woman. His thorn is her fruit.
    And vice-versa.

Joe Martyn Ricke

I know from one perspective, we really should be sorry about old
   Adam,
not to mention all the abuse Eve had to take all those years
(including quite a load of shit from Adam himself,
who delved out centuries of it while waiting for her to finish
   spinning their shrouds).
But still there's something so good, so fine, so deep down lovely
   about the revised version.
This greater Eve, this Avé girl, who took a lot more than an apple
   into her tender, young womb
and sprouted salvation, absurd and bloody and sweet and just in
   the
goddamned nick of time
(because four thousand and one years would have just been too
   much for anyone to take).

So I say, with all the saints and martyrs, whores and prophets,
You go girl Eve. You go on boyfriend Adam.
I love your free, flawed, passionate humanity.
With Harry Belafonte, I'm singing 'Day-Oh' for the
gracious feast you bought when you risked that crazy, rebel taste
   of truth.
Abel's lamb is served up to me, for me,
with a juicy apple in his mouth.
Blood still dripping from the snake bite.

Four Sinful Hymns for the Love of Saint Mary Magdalene

I. *At His Feet*

Sweet Mary Mags
loved Jesus's feet more than her lovely hair or diamonds
(I mean her tears).
And, as every good man but Augustine understands,
she really couldn't help but love her lovely hair.
God knows it's no great gift to give what's not loved much
to one you must love more.
What does it profit a girl,
she thought,
to gain the kingdom of heaven
but to lose his sole?

II. *Her Mother's Skin*

Magdalena cut herself
longing for something deeper
than the sex of centurions, publicans,
and guilt-ridden rabbis
who all paid extra for her silence.
The shit she'd eaten as a child
was all she knew of love
until the day, no doubt,
he scratched her name
into her mother's skin
(I mean the earth)
and said,
Close up your wounds
And drink from mine.

Joe Martyn Ricke

III. *Contemplation*

Martha cleaned things up for the love of God
and served pure kosher coffee to his Son,
for she knew the law and kept well the commandments.
To tell the Torah truth, she was goddamned sure of your duty as
    well.
Mary often skipped her lessons and skinny-dipped instead,
remembering only this from synagogue:
How lovely are the feet of those who bring good news.
. . . . .

Naturally, she recognized them right away,
dirty from his weary pilgrim road of love,
then knelt in the mud of her own tears and snot,
convulsing with a passion unknown to angels,
kissing, for hours, the sweet skin of the virgin's son–
her whoring done, her true love whispering her name.

IV. *Saint Mary's Spell*

Saint Mary sinned with all her senses–
she liked the look of her lovely hair reflected in a Roman bath,
craved the taste of pork on a pagan's lips,
sweet music could sway her into her dirty lover's arms,
whose touch she sometimes much more than endured,
and the human smell of sweat and love, like sage,
would suddenly make her moan with madness.
The dappled sunlight, the wind on her neck,
a dark young rabbi brushing against her in the street–
all these and more could set her skin to shivering with delight.

Until the day she was accused and
saw, for certain, she was going to die.
The crowd, the stones, the law she couldn't keep–

all cursed her now for what seemed sweet in the glamorous
   night.
When, in the whirligig of time, it came to pass,
that the whole damn world spun backwards on its base,
a strange man scratched rough magic in the earth, and behold–
while the righteous hung their heads like whores,
sweet Mary shone like Moses on the mountain,
her sinful eyes fixed on the fiery face of love,
where others saw but scandal.

Saint Mary Magdalene,
Pray for us.

Composed in Oxford, Feast of St. Mary Magdalene, 22 July 2013

Joe Martyn Ricke

The Pricking of Divine Love

On Enthroned Virgin (Child Missing), *Metropolitan Museum of Art*
Wood with traces of original polychromy (12ᵗʰ C.)

In this mean time, you
alone, enthroned, crowned,
seated at the right hand of the
stained glass window,
a busy picture full of busy men–
soldiers, some kings, a few demons–
thrusting their way, as usual, up into heaven,
the center of attention, they thought,
in their original French abbey
and, now, this busy room in the Met.

And you? Why still so still?
Alone, enthroned,
with your transplanted Scandinavian smirk–
so, what's the joke?
The sacred silent secret you aren't spilling?
Why not use your position,
the credit you've earned from that whole Twelfth-Century cult of
    . . .you,
a little more potently?

They look so stupid really, so, well,
medieval (as they say).
Chaining up St. Vincent.
Clutching their mighty, impressive swords.
Giving commands. Arranging martyrdoms.
Riding hard their sad-eyed mares.
Only to be outdone in the end by a long-haired angel in the top
    panel,
saving the day, *a caelo*, so to speak,
her upper torso hanging down,

her lower parts hidden up there behind the floral decorative
   frame
and the museum wall,
as if her angelic ankles were being held
by another angel and hers by another
all the way back up to you and your boy.

But that can't be. Not any more.
For when some Protestant vandal
removed that baby from your arms
(perhaps hoping that future generations would rise up and call
   you
just another extremely thin young woman of the Twelfth
   Century),
he took your hands as well.
Now, here,
in this dark city, in this warm room,
all that's left on the stubs of your two wooden arms
are holes where
then, there,
some lover of wood fashioned slender, polychromatic hands
   which,
I like to believe,
young girls would touch, wishing for shafts of grace,
showings of tenderness
in a cold, narrow, violent world.

Now, after fifteen years of visiting you,
and, in my way, venerating your bloodless wounds,
waiting for the piercing of the sword in my heart too,
I see, again, your other hole.
There, now,
the remains of a little wooden dowel
prick out from the folds of your faded blue robe.

Joe Martyn Ricke

Here, once, the maker
bolted to your womb
the absent sign of our absurd hope,
that a divine love could, would,
produce something more than man.

Seven Sevens and an Envoy for Juan Diego

Just last year Jill called and said
that nothing was finer or ever would be again
than the celebration of Our Lady of Guadalupe
in her local church, in Florida,
with the mariachis and the dancing.
Alright, I'm not sure she said dancing,
but this is not journalism; just shoot me when it is.

So I took a trek, I made a pilgrimage,
I mean, I left the Protestant comforts of home,
and drove fifty miles on 30 West to Warsaw, *Indiana that is,*
where the closest shrine to *Nuestra Señora* obviously was,
having read about it in the Catholic Directory, if there is such a
    thing,
and met at midnight with what felt like half a million Mexicans,
I mean at least a hundred of us standing and only one of us a
    very tall *gringo.*

I knew there would be mass, but in my ignorance
I knew so little how (so) much more to expect.
The singing, the children, the costumes, the flowers and families
    together at the shrine,
the processionals, the professionals, the prayers,
and, inconveniently, my heart ripped out of my chest and blood
    all over the pew.
My mother, my father, every love I've lost, *which pretty much
    includes them all,*
walking through the door, zombies too now, empty and bloody
    as hell,

finding me there. Then, together, parading down the aisle,
nuestros corazones heridos all turned to flowers in our hands.
We kneel together, music all around,

a song to the lady, the one Diego wrote,
Las Mañanitas, a birthday song for the precious one you love:
Despierta, mi bien, despierta, mira que ya amaneció
ya los pajarillos cantan, la luna ya se metió.

And it's not exactly a miracle that everything smells like roses,
since there are perhaps a New Year's Day parade's worth of
    them
piled together under her feet. And, yes, sometimes the celestial
    music
is slightly out of tune or the trumpets are just obviously showing
    off.
But it really doesn't matter about the roses or the guitars or the
    outfits
because you find yourself mumbling,
I've been bleeding a long time. Such a long long time.

And it goes without saying that this is the lady
with eyes like the western ocean and scars like *Barranca del Cobre*
who once said, 'you may touch my feet my pilgrim
but my thighs belong to *Padre Nuestro en los cielos*,'
who fed you berries by the road by the river your sorrows
    looking up into the dream of her face
by the mountain by your childhood by the constellations,
who even now weeps for your loneliness.

And then, so as not to die here,
you get up from the kneeler and retrace your hungry steps,
go forward for the bread, though they're stingy with the wine.
After, in the unfinished basement, you share *tamales* and *abuelita*
    chocolate and dancing
with folks you swear you've seen before.
It's clear they knew your father better than you did, though they
    were born after he died.
For they knew to call him *Carlos*, which you were not allowed to
    say.

Envoy

Adios, then, Juan Diego, but you know now where you are if not
   yet who you are,
and, perhaps, at least a little, why you came this way.
To bear witness, to these, *los campesinos preciosos*,
each with a message from the lady,
for the powers that be, for the white priests in dark robes–
the future is flowers
hiding in a poor man's cloak.

*This poem assumes some knowledge of the appearance of Our Lady of
Guadalupe to St. Juan Diego in Tepeyac, Mexico (1531).*

Joe Martyn Ricke

Stigmata Madonna

These wounds are the world's wonders.
Not a problem for professionals to fix,
not a question for asking, or for answers.

  Not a question, but a quest in skin,
  which tangled tortured love bid her do or die,

  a matching set of sorrowful mystery doors,
  scarred signs that stand for nothing but themselves.

Mouths that say, *awake*.
That sing, *attend*.
That shout, *now suck your fill of holiest human blood;*
and don't dare ever cease from this your thirstiest feeding.

See:
from her head, her hands, her womb, her wounds,
another bloody lover waiting to be born.

Hannah Stone

for Hannah-Freya
all good wishes
from another Hannah!

   The invitation to contribute to this anthology has prompted a
fruitful re-evaluation of my poetic techniques and sources. My
professional life as a Medievalist finds expression in the form
and content of my poetry. Geographically, my Medievalism is
Eastern rather than Western: temporally, it is a hybrid of Late
Antique and turn of the first Millennium. In my professional life
I am employed, *inter alia*, as a Reader in Eastern Christianity.
Here my research focuses on the spirituality of the most ancient
of Christianities, the 'orthodoxy' which was shared by all
Christians before denominational fragmentation. Particular
prompts to my poetry are the practice in the early Syrian church
of expressing theology through poetry, in which synaesthesia
featured prominently. The fourth century Saint Ephrem was the
greatest of the 'poet theologians'; he composed homilies in verse,
with refrains for the audience to sing. He wrapped the doctrine
in complex poetic forms, with vivid imagery. The Syrian church
expressed itself in metaphor, even to the extent of translating the
words confessing the Incarnation of Jesus Christ as 'he was
clothed in the body,' a phrase which inspired me to write an
entire book on the topic. Early Syrian Christianity sees the
natural world as a witness to God's power almost as important
as the written testaments. Whilst rarely focussing
unambiguously on Christian doctrine, my poetry celebrates the
synergy of the created world and the humans who inhabit it,
especially where I see evidence of a landscape worked by and for
the benefit of communities. This underpins poems such as
'Akoimetoi' and 'Credo.'
   Another area of my academic research is the mid-Byzantine
church of Constantinople at the turn of the first Millennium, a
colourful and quirky world which yoked sacred and secular
values in a complex manner. Juxtaposing that milieu to the
mundane demands and activities of modern, western, suburban
family life also yielded some poetry, including 'Silence in Court'

and 'St Deniol's Library,' which are not included here but may be found in my pamphlet.[12]

Latterly, a job with the Centre for the Study of Christianity and Culture has entailed research into the history of art and architecture and community life of English Cathedrals. This has spawned a large number of poems for me, often of an ekphrastic nature, and 'found' elements have provided prompts. The illustration in the guidebook to Exeter cathedral of a fine ginger cat emerging from a circular hole cut in the door of the tower delighted me; what a very practical solution to ridding the church of vermin of the rodent variety. In light-hearted homage to the powerful 'voice' of the inanimate cross in *The Dream of the Rood*, I gave this cat a voice in 'Square Peg'; an irreverent one which comments on the shenanigans within the church which employs him. In 'Book of Hours,' it is the scriptorium and the manuscript which have a 'voice.' The archaeological rarity of the well-preserved boots belonging to the 'Worcester Pilgrim' invited a poetic response.

My practice of interleaving cultural allusions, juxtaposing ancient and modern and using borrowed 'voices' has not fully satisfied my intentions in achieving the task set for this collection. Long before I became a church historian I read English Literature and Language at the University of London and was captivated by British medieval literature. Recently I began to revisit the forms and idioms of medieval poetry, aiming to avoid pastiche. I used alliteration in the relatively modern form of a prose poem ('Passibility') and revived the medieval troubadour form of the sestina for some dark pondering on the latest war in Gaza, which was imminent when I visited Jerusalem in June 2014. 'Eyeless in Gaza' uses as an inter-text to this contemporary situation a prayer by Aurelius Clemens Prudentius, set to music by the British Russian Orthodox composer John Tavener (d. 2013) which I recorded with a choir

---

[12] Hannah Stone, *Perfect Timing* (Leeds Createspace: Wordspace, 2014), 22-3 and 16-17.

recently.[13] I also began to translate Middle English texts, bearing in mind Edward Fitzgerald's comment: 'But at all Costs, a Thing must live: with a transfusion of one's own worse Life if he can't retain the Original's better. Better a live Sparrow than a stuffed Eagle.'[14] From a much longer prose original by Richard Rolle of Hampole, I selected material for 'The Nature of the Bee,' capturing the flavour of didactic exhortatory writing from the fourteenth century. Perhaps all poetry is a translation of sorts; an honouring of the language already used by others, re-crafted to new ends. This contribution is dedicated to my mother, Elizabeth Dixon, a fellow Medievalist and poet.

---

[13] 'Take Him Earth, for Cherishing', on St Peter's Singers, *One Equal Music*, 2014.

[14] Letter from Edward Fitzgerald to E.B. Cowell, 27 April, 1959, on his translation of the *Rubáiyát of Omar Khayyám*.

95   *Hannah Stone*

Akoimetoi

Their vigilance is not willed by greed
like the child wakeful on Christmas Eve.
It does not resemble the pounding pulse
of one who times the death rattle of a friend.

They watch for invisible gates to open,
waiting with the endurance of streams
trickling their muddy trails under walls,
or the persistence of dawn sliding aside
the drapes of night to uncover new paleness;
they lift hollow heads to track clouds scurrying
across a sky now bright, dark, starfilled.

They have become elemental;
ether clings to their spare frames,
bones already half spirit,
fingers flaring into holy flame.
Stylites decompose into rocky stems
over which lichen's bright shawl,
century by century, crawls.

*Akoimetoi: the unsleeping ones. A title given to desert hermits who
reputedly extended their ascetic discipline to renouncing sleep.*

The Worcester Pilgrim's Boots

The photo shows a skeleton
stretched alongside a measuring rod,
terminating at one end with an absence
in place of a skull,
at the other by knee high boots
splayed at ten to two.

I examine his boots.

Page 13 of the guidebook
offers a helpful diagram of the left one,
flattened like roadkill,
with numbered corners like tabbed paper dolls.
It details the parts – the vamp, the rand,
the heel stiffener and the sole.
It numbers the stitches per centimetre,
distinguishes tunnel stitch from whip stitch.
Evidence shows he did not die in these boots,
this un-named pilgrim,
and that he wore no hose
when he was dressed for burial.

No proofs are offered of how it felt
to walk in these boots. Did he stoop
for his cockleshell on an Essex beach
or a sunbaked strand? For what sins
was he atoning? Was he a spiritual mercenary,
accepting coins to erode his joints
as he erased the misdemeanours of a brother?
And the wounds – 'perhaps from arrows' –
Lacrimis Christi! Did he hope for stigmata,
or were these the honourable badges
of a true penitent? Decades of journeying are marked

Hannah Stone

in his worn right shoulder, which shows
just how he grasped his iron-tipped staff
to assist an ascent of some hill or other.

He must have noted the nigglesome stone beneath his heel
as, humbly, he waited in line for his dole.
But whether it was Spanish sun or English snow
which finished him off, we cannot know.

Pilgrim, peering into the glass case,
of your mercy, a prayer, or, if you will,
a candle to light him home.

The Nature of the Bee

Found/translated poem from Richard Rolle of Hampole, d. 1349

See the industrious bee, how she preserves the honey of pure life with sweetest grace. This is her first quality, that she is never still, but like the righteous man who is ever at his prayers, she busies herself with God's work. And he who is idle will find the devil corrupts his honey with worms, and fills his soul with bitterness. Such men are so weighted with cares of kin they cannot arise into the life of Christ Jesu. And this is the bee's second quality; that she takes just a little earth on her lacy wings, that she be not lightly raised too high by the airy wind. This earth resembles the humility of virtuous men, who shun the puff of vanity and pride, disregarding the clamour of sibling and stranger. And clean-living men, keeping the commandments in good conscience, have other virtues; they are unsullied by filthy sins and lusts. Just so the bee, who keeps her wings ever bright and clean, that she may fly straight to the love and contemplation of God.

Passibility

Let's say it was a sparrow, high above the heads of stalled travellers, that fistful of feathers flying north/south or maybe east/west. God knows where you really are in an airport. Somehow it must have dodged all human checks and curtailments, charting a circle of hell where the foetid fog from discarded food could not escape; no breath of un-recycled air could enter your lungs. It mapped a steady course through the canopy's metal frets. Maybe its DNA remembered the sparrow Bede borrowed to show the transience of human existence; a calm moment for the bird darting from one end of the hall to the other, then shooting out into the epistemological ignorance of the winter night, entering the historian's cloud of unknowing. It is winter in Newark, too. It's a toss-up between these two icons of illusory freedom: the ground-bound giant with its winking wings on the snowy runway, and this small brown bird who's got into the departure lounge but cannot find its way out.

Eyeless in Gaza

"Ask for this great deliverer now and find him
Eyeless in Gaza, at the mill with slaves."
(Milton, *Samson Agonistes* 1.40, 1671.)

The Via Dolorosa puts its shutters up. Boys
swarm down the steps in the waning light.
The day's heat seeps into red earth.
Across the valley, gunmen take aim, and fire,
sculpting with missiles an urban ruin:
take it, earth, for cherishing.

Take these young men and cherish them.
Eyal, Nafthali, Gilead – just boys
in the wrong place, squinting into sunlight,
now corpses concealed by a scattering of earth.
Rachel weeps for her children; grief fires
her heart. She rages against ruin.

They are noble even in their ruin,
each of these bodies brought for cherishing:
Shadrach, Meshach, Abednego, holy boys,
fearless of the furnace's burning light.
Their great faith earthing them,
they strode into the fire.

Hananiah, Azariah, Mishael seized the fire,
scorched the hatred, ruined it.
Allah, Yehovah, take and cherish them.
Prayer is better than sleep, boys,
brothers, calls the muezzin, daylight
dropping from heaven, prostrate on earth.

Gaza's murdered fall on baked earth,
their lost names merging like flames under shellfire
that renders their homeland a ruin.
Foraging on beaches, or cherishing
their pigeons on the roof, girls' and boys'
last moments flare in shameful spotlight.

At dusk, all hail the gladdening light;
invoke divine peace on everyone's earth.
Whichever God you serve, he's not in the fire
or earthquake, but in a small voice whispered to the ruined
city, huddled in arms that cherish
the broken limbs of a nation's boys.

Great deliverer, this earth you shaped from light
is ruined with shellfire, by your creation, man.
Hold back your boys; let them show cherishing.

Book of Hours

Layering two scripts together in midlife
creates a palimpsest of desire
where your tight cursive lingered round
my looping hand –
until the season when you awoke,
and scratched out the manuscript
we were co-authoring, and
with a sharp click, snapped shut
the gilt clasp on the tender vellum
of our first draft.

As the seasons cycle, I decide that next time
I'm tempted to transcribe a chapter
in the book of amours, I'd fare better
fooling around with some rude marginalia
like this priapic burgomeister, leering up
from the tail-end of 'September'
(spilling his cornucopia suggestively
at the foot of a vigorous – if leafless – tree),
his conk irreverently resembling the Duc de B's
and his brown hood slumped round his dewlap
in a manner which recalls Brother Sophronius,
about whose probity the Abbot, nightly, grieves.

Hannah Stone

Square Peg

The mice are the worst. Rats,
you can get your head round
(if you accept they're vicious brutes
with no morals, and bad breath to boot),
but mice – devious little bastards
and so many of the buggers!
Just as you clamp down on one,
up pops another, between the curls
of the bellrope: you'd swear
they were laughing at you.
    Ok, so I'm getting on,
and losing that tooth hasn't improved my looks
(not that the verger's tabby minds a jot)
but I'm still up to the job –
that penny a week to keep me in scraps
is well worth the candle. Talking of which,
ha! The candle ends those vermin chew –
scores of them – and don't get me started
on how they soil the purificators;
though why the sacristan leaves them
in the tower is beyond me, when
there's that fine linen-fold press for storage.
    The tales I would tell if only I could speak,
not just the messed up linen
but how he carries on with Mistress Anne
from the bakehouse. Fresh muffins, my arse!
Any fool can see what he's after
(though when you see how enticingly
they rise above her bodice,
I s'pose muffin's as good a word as any
for those bubbies.)
    Sometimes I think I'm wasted here,
a cathedral rodent catcher in a Mercian city.
That hole in the tower door

isn't a bit too tight for my lean flanks,
but it's getting to be quite a stretch down
to the step, the stone slab that takes you
into the cavernous barn of a place,
thronged with pilgrims and stallholders,
not to mention the pomp and circumstance –
barely a minute's peace till dusk!
    And another thing – I suspect
they're dissenters. Where will it end?

Hannah Stone

Credo

Chalcedon, Golden Horn. Anno Domini 451.
The Church Fathers are fed up;
their stiff robes chafe; their doctrines
don't sit comfortably, either.
Cyril's ghost wags a gnarled finger at Nestorius,
who's suffering from indigestion, even in the afterlife.
Spectres of Egyptian monks lay down their cudgels.

Unforgiving heat; unyielding diatribes;
the scribe flexes his cramped wrist.
An impartial slave flips the fan languidly.
His throat's so dry he cannot summon spit
to shift the fly climbing his thin, brown shin.
On palace roofs, bright-winged birds heckle.

A freeman clocks the whirring insect
with dispassion: he's in the wrong gathering,
but waits to see if there are seeds of Dharma
to be picked from this Christological squabble.
He flicks through a mental catalogue of sutra,
alights on the Metta-Sutta: loving kindness.

Long Preston, May time, round about now.
The sunrise cranks up an ambitious spread,
suggests its warmth might raise the pearly haze.
A walker out for an early stroll observes
layers of green valleys unveiling themselves;
disturbs the midges crowning a cowpat,
thinks – they've missed a bit, these holy men.

They've failed to grasp that some believe
that every day should offer glimpses
of hillsides, unfolding between meadows
and English attempts at cloudless skies.
We may not yearn for uncontested truths
shackling divine power with human rules,
but rather wait for rainfall's cleansing grace,
hope dry stone walls protect both sheep and man,
and know that birdsong heals.

Hannah Stone

About the Poets

Jane Beal, PhD writes poetry, fiction, and creative non-fiction as well as works of literary scholarship. She is the creator of more than a dozen poetry collections, including *Sanctuary* (Finishing Line Press, 2008) and *Rising* (Wipf & Stock, forthcoming 2015), as well as three recording projects: *Songs from the Secret Life, Love-Song*, and with her brother, saxophonist and composer Andrew Beal, *The Jazz Bird*. She has written *John Trevisa and the English Polychronicon* (ACMRS/Brepols, 2012), edited *Illuminating Moses: A History of Reception from Exodus to the Renaissance* (Brill, 2014), and with Mark Bradshaw Busbee, co-edited both *Translating the Past: Essays on Medieval Literature* (ACMRS, 2013) and *Approaches to Teaching the Middle English Pearl* (MLA, forthcoming). She has served as a professor at Wheaton College and Colorado Christian University, teaching literature and creative writing, and as a midwife in the U.S., Uganda, and the Philippines. She currently teaches at the University of California, Davis. To learn more, see http://sanctuarypoet.net.

Jane Chance is the Andrew W. Mellon Distinguished Professor Emerita in English at Rice University and a recent recipient of an honorary doctorate of letters from Purdue University. She has published twenty-two books on medieval literature and medievalism and received Guggenheim and NEH Fellowships, among other awards and prizes. Her book of poems, *Only Begetter*, was published by White Violet Press in 2014. Her poetry has appeared (also under the name J.C. Nitzsche) in *Antigonish Review, Ariel, Dalhousie Review, Icarus* (Trinity College Dublin), *Kansas Review, The Literary Review, Lyric, New America, Nimrod, Poet Lore, Primavera, Quartet, Southern Humanities Review,* and *Wascana Review* and other journals, and reprinted in the *Anthology of Magazine Verse and Yearbook of American Poetry.* Selected as a Juried Poet for the 2014 Houston Poetry Festival, she has been featured poet at Inprint and at several universities and art galleries in the Houston bay area and was juried into Marge Piercy's 2014 Poetry Intensive.

Pam Clements has been a professor of English at Siena College in Albany, New York, since 1988. She has also taught at The College of Charleston, in Charleston, South Carolina. As is commonplace in small liberal arts colleges, she wears several hats, teaching not only medieval courses such as Chaucer and Arthurian literature, but also History of the English Language, courses on literature of the fantastic, and more recently, creative writing. She has published on Old English sermons and wisdom literature and on contemporary medievalism. A founding member of *MEMO: Medieval Electronic Media Organization*, she co-edited, with Carol Robinson, *Neomedievalism in the Media: Essays on Film, Television, and Electronic Games* (Mellen, 2012). Her poems and essays have appeared in the literary journals *Kalliiope, The Baltimore Review, The Pacific Review, The Palo Alto Review*, and *Earth's Daughters*, among others. Her book of poems, *Earth Science* (The Troy Book Makers) was published in 2013.

Oz Hardwick is a writer, photographer and occasional musician, based in York (UK). Oz has been widely published in journals, anthologies and other media, and his fifth poetry collection, *The Ringmaster's Apprentice*, was published by Valley Press (Scarborough) in October 2014. He is co-author, with Amina Alyal, of *Close as Second Skins* (Beaworthy: Indigo Dreams Publishing, 2015) and has edited several collections. Oz has performed his work, both solo and in collaboration with a variety of writers and musicians, in Europe, the USA, and throughout the UK. As Paul Hardwick, he is Professor of English and Programme Leader for English and Writing at Leeds Trinity University. He is the author of *English Medieval Misericords: The Margins of Meaning* (Woodbridge: Boydell, 2011), and has published extensively on medieval art and literature, medievalism, and myth. www.ozhardwick.co.uk

M. Wendy Hennequin is a poet, song writer, and story-teller who performs many of her creative works with other performers in the U.S. and Canada. Some of her poetic translations were performed as part of a complete presentation of *Beowulf* by an international troupe of story-tellers in 2011 In her guise as an associate professor of English at Tennessee State University (Nashville, Tennessee), she has published and presented on various Old and Middle English texts and on pedagogy. One of her most recent articles, '*Beowulf* and World Literature I' (*Old English Newsletter* 44:3, 2013), discusses the melding of poetry and translation (and her vocations of poet and teacher) in the classroom.

A.J. Odasso's poetry has appeared in a number of strange and wonderful publications, including *Sybil's Garage*, *Mythic Delirium*, *Jabberwocky*, *Cabinet des Fées*, *Midnight Echo*, *Not One of Us*, *Dreams & Nightmares*, *Goblin Fruit*, *Strange Horizons*, *Stone Telling*, *Farrago's Wainscot*, *Through the Gate*, *Liminality*, *inkscrawl*, and *Battersea Review*. Her début collection, *Lost Books* (Flipped Eye Publishing, 2010), was nominated for the 2010 London New Poetry Award and for the 2011 Forward Prize, and was also a finalist for the 2011 People's Book Prize. Her second collection with Flipped Eye, *The Dishonesty of Dreams*, was released in August of 2014. Her two chapbooks, *Devil's Road Down* and *Wanderlust*, are available from Maverick Duck Press. She holds degrees from Wellesley College and the University of York (UK). She has been Senior Poetry Co-Editor at *Strange Horizons* magazine since 2012. She currently lives in Boston with her partner and a tank full of inquisitive freshwater fish. You can find her online at ajodasso.livejournal.com.

Joe Ricke is a teacher, actor, director, singer-songwriter, musician, and writer who lives in rural Indiana, USA. His work includes dozens of dramatic productions and performances, mostly Shakespeare and late medieval drama; two albums of music – *World without Synthesizers* and *Little Clarissa and Other Stories*; scholarly articles on English literature – most recently

'The Framing of the Shrew' for a volume on *Teaching Taming of the Shrew* (MLA, 2013); and numerous poems, essays, and reviews. He has also recorded several medieval works for The Chaucer Studio. He studied for his Ph.D. in English Literature with Jane Chance at Rice University. He has played Satan in York Minster, played Herod in the crypt at Canterbury, played his songs on stage at Luckenbach, Texas, and, most important, has led a sing-along at the International Congress on Medieval Studies for the last ten years or more.

Hannah Stone is a poet, academic writer and singer born in London but resident in Leeds for many years. She has sold paintings and drawings, been recorded and broadcast singing in various choirs, and currently performs poetry with half a dozen groups in Yorkshire and beyond. In the last year she has had over 50 poems published, including for *Caught in the Net* 130, *Hinterland Journal of Contemporary Poetry*, *Poesia Indignada*, and, with Gill Lambert and Maria Preston, the collection, *An After Dinner's Sleep* (Wordspace/Indigo Dreams Publishing, 2015). As Hannah Hunt, she is Reader in Eastern Christianity at Leeds Trinity University, under which guise she has published many articles and chapters in the field of Late Antique and Mid-Byzantine Church history, especially its spirituality. Monographs include *Joy-Bearing Grief* (Leiden: Brill, 2004) and *Clothed in the Body* (Aldershot: Ashgate, 2012). Forthcoming monographs in 2015/6 are for Wipf and Stock (US) and Brill.

Acknowledgements

Jane Chance: 'The Château de Comper' appeared as a juried poet selection in *Houston Poetry Fest 2014 Anthology* (Houston: Houston Poetry Fest, 2014); 'The Savior of Worm Hall' originally appeared in *Nimrod* 21 (fall-winter 1976), under the name of J. C. Nitzsche, and was reprinted in Jane Chance, *Only Begetter* (Torrance, CA: White Violet Press, 2014); 'Migration' appeared in *Round Top Festival Institute Presents the Thirteenth Annual Poetry at Roundtop Festival Hill 2014 Anthology* (Round Top: Poetry at Round Top Festival, 2014); and 'Humors for Ash-Wednesday,' originally appeared in *Bard Literary Magazine* 5:1 (Fall, 1965) as the Kneale Award for Poetry at Purdue University, but was revised into its current form in *Only Begetter*.

Pam Clements: 'Wodewose' appeared in Gay Baines and Mary Ann Eichelberger, *Celebrations* (July Literary Press, 2006) and in Pam Clements, *Earth Science* (The Troy Book Makers, 2013). 'Vivien/Merlin' appeared in *Bardsong (2004)* and in *Earth's Daughters* (2013).

Oz Hardwick: 'The Green Man Awakes' and 'The Seafarer's Return' appeared in Oz Hardwick, *The Illuminated Dreamer* (Kingsbridge: Oversteps, 2011); 'The Green Man Awakes' also appeared as the title poem in *The Green Man Awakes*, ed. Rose Drew (Stairwell Books, 2009); 'Annunciation' appeared in *Hildegard*, ed. Gabriel Griffin (Orta San Giulio: Wyvern, 2014); an earlier version of 'True Thomas' appeared in *The Dawn Treader* 6 (2009).

A.J. Odasso: 'Your last word on earth' has previously appeared in *Star*Line* 38.2.

Hannah Stone: 'Book of Hours' and 'Square Peg' appeared in *Perfect Timing*, a self-published pamphlet which was the inaugural volume of the imprint Wordspace, created as an MA submission for the Leeds Trinity University Creative Writing programme (now taken on by Indigo Dreams Publishing) and available via Createspace (Amazon, 2014).

Other anthologies and collections available from Stairwell Books

First Tuesday in Wilton	Ed. Rose Drew and Alan Gillott
The Exhibitionists	Ed. Rose Drew and Alan Gillott
The Green Man Awakes	Ed. Rose Drew
Fosdyke and Me and Other Poems	John Gilham
frisson	Ed. Alan Gillott
Gringo on the Chickenbus	Tim Ellis
Running With Butterflies	John Walford
Late Flowering	Michael Hildred
Scenes from the Seedy Underbelly of Suburbia	Jackie Simmons
Pressed by Unseen Feet	Ed. Rose Drew and Alan Gillott
York in Poetry Artwork and Photographs	Ed. John Coopey and Sally Guthrie
Rosie and John's Magical Adventure	The Children of Ryedale District Primary Schools
Her House	Donna Marie Merritt
Taking the Long Way Home	Steve Nash
Chocolate Factory	Ed. Juliana Mensah and Rose Drew
Skydive	Andrew Brown
Still Life With Wine and Cheese	Ed. Rose Drew and Alan Gillott
Somewhere Else	Don Walls
Sometimes I Fly	Tim Goldthorpe
49	Paul Lingaard
Homeless	Ed. Ross Raisin
Satires	Andy Humphrey
The Ordinariness of Parrots	Amina Alyal

For further information please contact rose@stairwellbooks.com

www.stairwellbooks.co.uk